LOOK WHAT THE

Lord

HAS DONE!

LOOK WHAT THE
Lord
HAS DONE!

REMEMBERING REMARKABLE EXPERIENCES

DIANE HEMPHILL

authorHOUSE®

AuthorHouse™ LLC
1663 Liberty Drive
Bloomington, IN 47403
www.authorhouse.com
Phone: 1-800-839-8640

Published by AuthorHouse 12/21/2013

ISBN: 978-1-4918-3284-4 (sc)
ISBN: 978-1-4918-3283-7 (e)

Library of Congress Control Number: 2013920258

Contents

Dedication

To my husband, Larry, the love of my life. He is my loving companion, my encourager, and my strong arm to lean on. He was also my pastor for almost 36 years. Words could never express how much I love him!

To our three sons, Steve, Chris, and Scott, whom I greatly love and cherish. They have grown up to be fine Christian young men, and they have been such a blessing to us! They have seen and experienced the many wonderful things that the Lord has done in our lives.

To my mother, Rachel Moss, whom I deeply love and appreciate. Also, in loving memory of my dad, Charles V. Moss, whom I deeply loved and appreciated as well. My parents were married for 72 years! They took me to church and taught me by their godly example how to love God and serve Him with all my heart.

PREFACE

Remembering is a vital part of our Christian journey. In the pages of this book, I have endeavored to remember the incredible things that the Lord has done in my life and in the lives of my family.

The idea of writing this book came while I was praying in our spare bedroom at the parsonage of the Bryson City Church of God in Bryson City, North Carolina. While on my knees, I started feeling impressed to get up and write down ideas for different chapters as the Lord would remind me of things He had done in our lives. I would write down a few ideas for chapters and go back to praying. Then I would feel led to write down a few more ideas and go back to praying again. This went on for a good while, until I had written down 36 things about which to write. I was so excited! Since that time, I have recorded many more amazing experiences.

As we continued on in pastoral ministry, I managed to squeeze in some time for writing, along with working as a substitute teacher in North Carolina during some of those years. Then after Larry retired, I wrote some in between my work as a Sales Representative at The School Box and as a substitute teacher for the Paulding County School District in Georgia. It has been my dream for many years to be able to write books, as well as magazine and newspaper articles. I also enjoy writing poems and gospel songs.

I want to thank my husband for his patience while I spent many hours writing and typing the pages of this book. It has been a joy to write about some of the many things the Lord has done for our family.

Most of all, I thank God for His help and strength during the writing of this book.

ACKNOWLEDGMENTS

Here is where I give heartfelt thanks to those who helped with this book.

I gratefully acknowledge our son, Chris Hemphill, for editing the material you are about to read.

Also, thanks to our son, Scott Hemphill, for helping me with getting the manuscript prepared. His wife, Whitney, helped as well with editing when this book was in the early stages of preparation.

I also wish to thank my husband, Larry, for his understanding and encouragement while I completed this task.

I must not fail to acknowledge the team at AuthorHouse for their timely work in printing this book.

INTRODUCTION

The pages of this book are intended to show what marvelous things God has done—not back in Bible days—but in the everyday lives of individuals in these modern times.

My husband, Larry, and I have been in the ministry for 45 years as of this writing. I wanted to share with others what God has done in our lives and in the lives of our children as we journeyed through life in the work of the ministry. Through the years, countless people were saved, sanctified, and filled with the Holy Ghost in our services. Also, lives were changed and needs were met. We thank God for allowing us to work in His vineyard and for all the wonderful people with whom we worked in each church we pastored. There were good times and bad times, but God has helped us (and is still helping us) all the way.

As you will see, many times God would reveal things to us ahead of time when we would seek Him about His will for our lives, or He would guide us and lead us in miraculous ways as we would pray and fast for direction. This is not a new thing. One of our Sunday school lessons entitled "The Arsenal of Prayer" reads, "There are many examples of fasting and praying in the Bible, and scriptures tell of the good results brought by this spiritual discipline. Fasting and praying, if practiced with a sincere desire to draw near to God and have His will done in our lives, can be effective."[1]

Please understand that I am sharing these incidents in our lives to bring glory to God, and not to bring any glory to myself or my family. I just feel a great need to tell the world what God has done and what He can do. Moses didn't keep quiet about how God opened up the

---

[1] Black, Daniel L., *Winter 2012-2013 Adult Student Guide*; Pathway Press, Cleveland, TN.; p. 63.

Red Sea and let all the Israelites walk through the middle of it on dry ground, and then drowned their enemies by closing the sea on top of them! Neither should we keep quiet when God performs great miracles in our lives.

So when you read these pages and wonder, "How did God show them ahead of time what would happen?" or "How can God reveal to people which way to take or what decision to make?"—just remember that He will do the same for you if you will pray and fast and seek God with all your heart.

E. M. Bounds once said in his book, *The Weapon of Prayer*, "It is the spiritual man who prays, and to praying ones God makes His revelations through the Holy Spirit."[2]

Sometimes the Lord has given us what we call "signs," showing us certain words or objects, or putting things in front of our faces so many times that we would take notice of them and write them down. Then later, He would show us why that object or that word had significance. It was His way of giving us the assurance that we were in the right place or that we were in His will. I know this sounds strange to some people. I am concerned that some who will read this book will misunderstand about "seeing things over and over again." Just remember that God has to be the One who gives you these signs, and you should never act on an impression or a sign unless God confirms it to you definitely. Even our children would laugh and say things about the "signs" Momma saw ahead of time, misunderstanding the fact that God does work that way!

It is through the work of the Holy Ghost. The Gifts of the Spirit are given by God to those who seek for them. They are used by God to show things that were not known before. I want to stress that all of the nine wonderful Gifts of the Spirit are supernatural. They are listed in the Bible in I Corinthians 12: 8-10.

We are admonished in the Scriptures to "covet earnestly the best gifts" (I Corinthians 12:31) and to "desire spiritual gifts" (I Corinthians 14:1). The Gifts of the Spirit are for power, and all of them are miraculous.

It has been said that these Gifts overflow one another. They harmonize and merge, and you may not always be able to tell

---

[2] Bounds, E. M., *The Weapon of Prayer*, (Grand Rapids, MI: Revell, 1931), p. 84.

where one begins and the other ends. As you may know, the Word of Knowledge and the gift of the Word of Wisdom are used by God to reveal things. In his book, *The Gifts of the Spirit*, Harold Horton explains the purpose of these two gifts. He says: "The Word of Knowledge is the revelation of past happenings or of things existing or events taking place in the present. The Word of Wisdom is the revelation of the Purpose of God concerning people, things or events in the future or looking to the future . . . . The Word of Wisdom may thus be manifested through the audible divine Voice. It may also be manifested by angelic visitation, by dream or vision, or through the spiritual Gifts of Prophecy, or Tongues and Interpretation."[3]

When you read the following account of our lives, remember that God does work that way (through signs and wonders). Notice the words of Nebuchadnezzar, king of Babylon, recorded in Daniel 4:2 & 3: "I thought it good to shew the signs and wonders that the high God hath wrought toward me. How great are his signs! And how mighty are his wonders!" It has been such a blessing to see how God is so interested in our lives and how He loves to reveal things to us by signs and wonders. And remember—He will do the same for you!

> "He delivereth and rescueth, and he worketh signs and wonders in heaven and in earth . . ." (Daniel 6:27a).

> Diane Hemphill
> Powder Springs, Georgia

---

[3] Horton, Harold, *The Gifts of the Spirit*, (Assemblies of God Publishing House, 1966), p. 68.

"Great is the Lord, and greatly to be praised; and His greatness is unsearchable. One generation shall praise thy works to another, and shall declare thy mighty acts. I will speak of the glorious honour of thy majesty, and of thy wondrous works. And men shall speak of the might of thy terrible acts: and I will declare thy greatness. They shall abundantly utter the memory of thy great goodness, and shall sing of thy righteousness. The Lord is gracious, and full of compassion; slow to anger, and of great mercy. The Lord is good to all: and his tender mercies are over all his works. All thy works shall praise thee, O Lord; and thy saints shall bless thee. They shall speak of the glory of thy kingdom, and talk of thy power; to make known to the sons of men his mighty acts, and the glorious majesty of his kingdom."
Psalm 145: 3-12 (KJV)

CHAPTER ONE

HOW IT ALL BEGAN

To better acquaint you with our lives as pastor and pastor's wife, I will endeavor to tell you a little about our background.

I was the second of four children born to my parents, Charles Virlyn Moss and Rachel King Moss of Atlanta, Georgia. My sister, Brenda Powers, is a little older than me, and my brother, Jerry Moss, was two years younger than me. My youngest brother, David Moss, was born when I was eight years old.

My oldest brother, Jerry Charles Moss, was a 1971 graduate of Lee College and he was a good Christian young man. He went home to be with the Lord at the age of 24. His sudden death (in 1973) was caused by an inflammation of the heart muscle due to pneumonia, resulting in a heart attack. He was in the Naval Air Reserves in Texas when he passed away. Our family was devastated by his death, and, oh, how we miss him!

My dad recently went home to be with the Lord (April 3, 2013), after being very sick for about 5 months. We miss him so very much, but we are so thankful that the Lord let him live to be 89 years old. I am comforted by the assurance that he is now safe in the arms of Jesus.

My husband Larry was the first son born to his parents, Fulton Washington Hemphill and Geneva Lawrence Hemphill. Both of his parents have gone on to their reward. His family lived in Charlotte, North Carolina, when he was born and until he was about five years old. They lived in Toccoa, Georgia, until he was 11 years old, and then moved to Chamblee, Georgia, and lived there until he graduated from high school. After graduation, his family moved to Smyrna, Georgia. God brought him all the way from Charlotte to Atlanta so we could meet each other!

Larry has an older sister, Jane Radford, two younger brothers, Tommy Hemphill and Rev. Richard Hemphill, and a younger sister, Mary Grace Forrester. Another sister, Barbara, died shortly after birth.

I gave my heart and life to the Lord Jesus Christ when I was five years old. My mother led me to the Lord as we knelt beside my brother's bed. I received the baptism of the Holy Ghost when I was fourteen, at the Riverside Church of God in Atlanta, Georgia.

Larry and I met at the Riverside church. That was the church I had attended all my life. His family started coming to my church when he was a teenager. We were married June 23, 1962, just a few days after Larry graduated from John Marshall Law School.

We were active members of the Riverside church until we went into pastoral work in 1970.

The Lord has blessed us with three wonderful sons, Steve, Chris, and Scott. Steve graduated from Kennesaw State University with a degree in Business Administration. He is married to the former Adriana Agamez from Barranquilla, Colombia and they have one son, Mateo (age 12). They live on Siesta Key in Sarasota, Florida. Chris is a graduate of Lee University in Cleveland, Tennessee, and he received his Master's degree in Education from Shorter College in Rome, Georgia. He is married to the former Crystal Shepherd. They make their home in Rydal, Georgia (near Cartersville). Scott is married to the former Whitney Higginbotham and both of them graduated from Lee University. They reside in the suburbs of Pittsburg, Pennsylvania. They have three children—Lily Grace (age 8), Jonathan Locke (age 5), and Levi Bryant (age 3). Our children and grandchildren are so precious to us!

We have pastored sixteen churches through the years, located in Georgia, Florida, and North Carolina. We have often wondered why God led us from church to church, never staying more than four and a half years at any one place. It is sort of like the journey of the children of Israel. If our life's journey was recorded like the Israelites' wilderness journey was recorded in Numbers, chapter 33, it would read something like this:

"And these were the journeys of the Hemphill's who went forth out of Marietta, Georgia, and these are their journeys according to their goings out. They first went to Dawsonville, Georgia, and then they made their way to Buford, Georgia. They removed to Doraville, Georgia, going to Savannah, Georgia after that. They removed from Savannah and pitched at Shannon, Georgia, then ventured further to Sarasota, Florida. Next, they took their journey to Ringgold, Georgia and encamped there until they departed to Cornelius, North Carolina. After departing from Cornelius, they journeyed to Lacoochee, Florida and then on to Trenton, Georgia. After removing from Trenton, they journeyed to Melbourne, Florida, then to Hazelwood, North Carolina and after that, they encamped at Reidsville, North Carolina. When they departed from Reidsville, they journeyed to Bryson City, North Carolina, then to Cashiers, North Carolina and on to their encampment at Seagrove, North Carolina. After retiring from pastoral ministry in 2007, they now reside in Powder Springs, Georgia, preaching the gospel in various churches as God opens doors."

What a journey it has been! The Lord has led us every step of the way, and He has been with us to help us and to supply our every need. I must say that we don't regret a mile!

The following chapters will reveal just how the Lord led us and how He supplied our needs.

"Give unto the Lord the glory due unto his name; worship the Lord in the beauty of holiness" (Psalm 29:2).

CHAPTER TWO

THE PUZZLING DREAM

During the late 1960's, before we went into the ministry, I had a dream one night that puzzled me. I dreamed that someone had died, and I saw many details about the funeral home visitation and the funeral, but I couldn't figure out who had passed away.

In my dream, my husband and I went to Couch's Funeral Home near the church we had attended for years, (the Riverside Church of God in Atlanta) for the viewing of someone who had passed away. The casket was in a room on the right side of a hallway and was situated on the far side of the room. After we passed by the casket, we turned and saw a certain elderly lady from our church sitting near the casket. We spoke to her and went out of the room.

The details of the funeral were also plainly seen in my dream. Our church choir was dressed in black and white, and we marched through the upstairs hall of the Sunday School building and into the choir from the doors behind the choir section of our church. My husband and I were a part of that choir, and in my dream, we were in the choir (dressed in black and white), singing songs at the funeral of this unknown person.

The dream seemed so real, and I wondered what it could mean. Then about three days later, we received the sad news that our former pastor, Rev. J. D. Bright, had passed away. He had retired a few months before that, due to heart problems. We dearly loved this pastor and his wife, and we had been to visit them at their home on the

Church of God campground in Doraville, Georgia, during his time of illness.

When we received the news about his death, I knew then that my dream had been about him. But I was shocked when we visited the funeral home near the church, went into the room on the right that I had dreamed about, and passed the casket which was in the same spot as it was in my dream. After viewing the body, we turned and saw that same elderly lady sitting nearby, just as I had seen her in my dream. We spoke to her and went out of the room.

In preparation for the funeral, the choir director asked all of the choir members to sing at the funeral and he asked us to wear black and white. Just before the funeral, the choir gathered downstairs in the Sunday School department and marched upstairs and through the hall of the Sunday School building, entering the choir through the back doors of the choir section—just as I had seen in my dream. My husband and I were a part of the choir that day, and we sang the songs his family had requested. It was quite an experience living out all the details of a dream from three nights before! It was a sad time, but I was amazed that God would reveal to me in advance what He was about to do.

> "Oh, Lord God, thou hast begun to show thy servant thy
> greatness, and thy mighty hand: for what God is there
> in heaven or in earth, that can do according to thy great
> works, and according to thy might?" (Deuteronomy 3:24).

CHAPTER THREE

THE SEWING MACHINE MIRACLE

After we had been married about seven or eight years, and before we went into pastoral work, Larry bought me a portable sewing machine. I did some sewing for myself, but one day I felt led to make a dress for a lady from the Riverside Church of God, where we attended. This was going to be a surprise for her. I asked her daughter about her mother's dress size and then bought the material and other things to make the dress. I wanted it to be really pretty, so I chose some beautiful red material.

I proceeded to cut out the dress and set up the portable sewing machine on our kitchen table. I was so happy that I was finally going to get started sewing the dress. But when I pressed the foot pedal, the machine would not work. It had just been serviced, so we couldn't figure out why it wouldn't work. We tried everything we knew to do.

We then decided to pray over it! We prayed earnestly that the Lord would fix it somehow, so I could make the dress. When we finished praying, I pressed the pedal, and the machine worked perfectly! We rejoiced over such a quick and wonderful answer to our prayers!

After a few days, I finished the dress and gave it to the lady. She was so happy, and to my surprise, it fit her perfectly. She wore it to church many times. Thank God that He cares even about the little things that concern us.

".... I will help thee, saith the Lord ...." (Isaiah 41:14).

CHAPTER FOUR

AN UNEXPECTED BLESSING

One important part of my life has been my love for writing songs. Since 1970, the Lord has been giving me the words and tunes to gospel songs.

The first song He gave me was "What A Happy Time." I wrote it on a Monday morning after we had been in a wonderful revival service at the Mableton Church of God in Mableton, Georgia, on a Sunday night.

On that Monday morning, I prepared breakfast and started packing a school lunch for Steve. I started hearing a tune in my mind and then the words to a song came into my mind immediately. I remember that I was just bubbling over with joy from the blessing I had received the night before, and I felt compelled to stop what I was doing and write down the words to the song. In just a few minutes, I wrote three verses and a chorus to my first song. I felt God's anointing in a powerful way.

At that time, I was just learning to play the piano, but I picked out the tune with one finger, and kept it in my head until I could play all the harmony parts. Sadly, though, I put it in my piano stool for seven years! After the seven years, it seemed that the Lord started dealing with me to practice it and send it to Charles Towler, a music publisher that we knew at the Tennessee Music and Printing Company, to see if he would write the music for me. So I did, and he quickly wrote the music for me. In his letter that he sent along with the music sheet, he shocked me by asking if I wanted him to submit the song to the

Music Committee for review to see if they wanted to publish it in the next convention song book. Of course, I said "yes" and, to my great surprise, I soon received a contract for the song to be published in their yearly convention song book. What a thrill!

After that, the Lord started giving me more songs, and eventually I took lessons from a music professor at Shorter College in Rome, Georgia, for five months to learn how to write my own music. This helped me tremendously.

I remember praying one day on the floor with my face on the carpet, asking the Lord to give me a song to comfort people when they were grieving over the death of a loved one. Someone from our church had just passed away and I saw the grief and sorrow the family was experiencing. In just a short time, the Lord gave me the words and melody to the song "Jesus Really Cares."

The Lord gave me the words and music to the song "I'm Gonna Sail Away" just a short while later. I played it on my new organ and practiced it over and over. While in the kitchen preparing a meal a few days later, I found myself singing a brand new part to the song that I had never heard before. I was surprised! I immediately added that part to the end of the chorus, and it was a great improvement to the song. It was published exactly that way.

One night many years later, I was in bed, half asleep and very tired, when I began to hear a song in my mind, and it was so beautiful to me! I felt that I should get up and go to the keyboard and play the song (using my earphones, of course, so I wouldn't wake up my family). It was around one o'clock in the morning, and I finished writing the song around 2 a.m. That song was titled "Heaven's Happy Land."

Then, a few years ago, I dreamed that I was looking at the music to a certain song that we sometimes sang at our church. I saw the words and music to the first line only, and it seemed that the Lord was pointing to that line with His finger, instructing me to write a song using the same rhythm as that song, but using a totally different tune and, of course, different words. The next day, I found the music to that song, and immediately the Lord started giving me the words to write down and also the melody to a brand new song. That song is titled "Jesus Is With Me Everywhere I Go." A short time later, the McKameys recorded it.

Many of the songs I have written are about Heaven, but several of them are songs of comfort, encouragement, and hope. Some songs were inspired by Scripture verses or sermons, or by experiences I had gone through. Others were inspired by devotional articles I found in devotion books. I have found that some songs come quickly and other songs come as a result of long hours of hard work! But either way, God can use them to be a blessing to others.

Charles Towler barely knew me when I sent him my first song, but I will forever be grateful to him for helping me to get my songs published in song books, and for his encouraging comments all along by phone, letter, or E-mail.

I thank God for all He has done and trust that the songs He has given me (as well as those He may give me in the future) will be a blessing to people for years to come.

"I will praise the name of God with a song, and will
magnify him with thanksgiving" (Psalm 69:30).

CHAPTER FIVE

FASTING AND PRAYER BROUGHT AN ANSWER

After living in our first home in Smyrna, Georgia, for about five years, we bought a new home in Marietta, Georgia. Larry was going to Beulah Heights Bible College at night to earn a Bachelor's Degree in Religion. By this time, God had changed the direction of his life, from his desire to be a lawyer to being a minister! When he graduated from Bible College in the summer of 1970, we were excited about the prospect of pastoring a church somewhere, but no doors were opening. Churches were mentioned to us, but each time, another minister would be appointed there. Yet, we were confident that pastoring was the work the Lord wanted us to do.

We prayed, but still nothing happened. We both decided to fast for three days and pray earnestly for the Lord to open the door for us to pastor a church. Neither of us had ever fasted for three days, but we felt led to do it and we felt desperate enough to go without food for those three days. We went about our normal activities during those three days, but giving ourselves to extra prayer. Larry was working a full time job in Atlanta (in the insurance business) and I was busy with housework and taking care of our first son, Steve. He was four years old.

After a very short time, we received a phone call from the State Overseer asking us if we would be willing to go to pastor the Dawsonville Church of God in Dawsonville, Georgia. Of course, we said "yes" and we went for our first service soon after that, in October of 1970. The church didn't have a parsonage, so we drove about 65 miles each Sunday morning to preach, and then 65 miles back home late on Sunday nights after the evening service.

Eventually, we started having a service for children an hour before the regular Sunday evening service. I would tell "flash" stories from special books I had bought. The children loved it, and responded in a great way. They came to church eager to hear the Word of God, and then filled the altars at the end of the services, seeking God with all their hearts. Later on, we also started having Teen Time for the teenagers.

We spent our Sunday afternoons visiting our church members after a great lunch at someone's home. The families of the church took turns feeding us on Sundays.

I was just learning to play the piano, but they graciously put up with my playing when there was no one else there to play.

The church couldn't afford to pay our way to summer Camp Meeting, so they bought Larry a nice suit, and one of the ladies made two dresses for me. Someone else gave me some hosiery. We were thrilled to receive these things.

The services at Dawsonville were very good, with people saved, sanctified, and filled with the Holy Ghost. The Lord really blessed us during our 18 months there.

There will always be a special place in our hearts for the people at the Dawsonville church. They were a special group of people who went out of their way to show love to us and to help us during our time there.

"I will meditate also of all thy work, and talk of thy doings"
(Psalm 77:12).

CHAPTER SIX

LITTLE ANGELS ALL AROUND
THE ROOM

While pastoring our first church, we had a benefit singing for a little four-year old girl who lived in the community. She was scheduled to have open heart surgery in another state, and the doctors had only given her a 50/50 chance of surviving the surgery.

At the benefit singing, my husband asked everyone to come to the front one by one and pray over a cloth which had been anointed with oil. It was to be given to the little girl's parents to put on or near her during the surgery. When we prayed together that night for her, we really felt God's presence in a great way.

Several weeks later, my husband saw the little girl's dad and asked about her progress. He was happy to report that she came through the surgery just fine. He said she was supposed to stay in the hospital a long time, but was released much earlier than expected because she was doing so well. He said his daughter had told him that while she was in the hospital for the surgery, she saw little tiny angels floating all around the room, and one of them came and sat on her forehead! There is no limit to what my God can do!

"This is the Lord's doing; it is marvelous in our eyes"
(Psalm 118:23).

CHAPTER SEVEN

THE MESSAGE ON THE WALL

While we were pastoring a church in Buford, Georgia, the Lord gave me a vision one morning, just as I was waking up. On the wall of our bedroom, I saw a big screen with lights all around it, similar to what you would see in the dressing room of an actress. Then I saw words coming on the screen, one letter at a time, like it was being typed. The message was very plain and clear, and it contained only two sentences. It read: "Use your time wisely. Make good use of your time."

I was so astonished to see this, yet I knew in an instant that it was from God and I knew what He wanted me to do. You see, the Lord can see in the future, and He knew that we would be leaving that church to go to another one in a matter of a few short weeks.

I had been procrastinating about working on a special project that would benefit our church financially. One hundred recipes had been collected from the ladies of the church to make a nice cookbook to sell to their friends and family members. A representative from the publishing company had already worked with me in the community to get the necessary advertisements for the book. So, the only thing for me to do now was to type the 100 recipes and mail them in.

It seemed like such a monumental task for an expectant mother with morning sickness and constant headaches. I remember going back to bed many mornings, or just resting on the sofa for hours during the afternoon.

Diane Hemphill

After the Lord gave me the vision, I decided to start working the next morning, just as a secretary would, from 9:00 A.M. to 5:00 P.M. No matter how long it took, I was determined to get it done. And guess what? It only took two days!

A few weeks later, the Lord moved us to another church, but the church at Buford later benefited financially from the sale of the cookbooks. I use my copy of that cookbook every now and then, and when I pick it up, I am reminded of that early morning vision.

The message on that screen not only helped me then, but it has helped me all through my life. I learned how important it is to use my time wisely.

"I will praise thee, O Lord, with my whole heart; I will shew forth all thy marvelous works" (Psalm 9:1).

Chapter Eight

A MISSIONARY'S DISAPPEARANCE

In the early 1970's, while we were pastoring in Dunwoody, Georgia, we received word that a missionary friend of ours was missing. People everywhere were praying that he would be found alive. It was such a mystery, and it was so sad to know that his wife was in a foreign country not knowing whether her husband was dead or alive.

This was a wonderful missionary couple with whom we were acquainted, and they had been in India for many years. They would come to our home church at Riverside in Atlanta, Georgia, to speak in the services while they were on furlough. We prayed earnestly that the Lord would intervene and that he would be found.

Then, I had a dream one night that our missionary friend was found alive, and that he later came to preach for us at our church in Dunwoody. I wrote a letter to his wife telling her about my dream, hoping it would encourage her and give her hope.

A short time later, her husband was found alive, but he had amnesia and couldn't tell anyone what had happened to him or where he had been all that time. Both of them were brought back to the United States, and they moved into a house on the Church of God campground in Doraville, Georgia, which was not far from where we lived.

After our missionary friend recovered, my husband asked him to come and preach for us at our church. What a joy it was to see him alive and well and preaching in our church! We invited him to our home after church to eat a meal with us, and we enjoyed talking with him and having him as a guest at our house. Thank the Lord for the dream assuring us (and his wife and family) that he would be found. Also, we were thankful that the Lord had protected him and helped someone to find him. My God can do anything!

> "Call unto me and I will answer thee, and shew thee great
> and mighty things, which thou knowest not"
> (Jeremiah 33:3).

Chapter Nine

THE FROSTLESS REFRIGERATOR

Can angels fix a refrigerator? We believe they can! Here is what happened.

The ladies from the church we were pastoring in Dunwoody, Georgia, were having a bake sale at a little strip mall nearby. My husband and I were there to help sell the baked goods that day. A retired minister and his wife from our church walked up on the sidewalk and started looking in the window of an appliance store. We went over to talk to them and they told us they were looking for a refrigerator. Their refrigerator had quit working, and she was trying to find one that was frost-free. She had some heart trouble and wanted one that was easy to maintain.

My husband asked them if they would be interested in a good refrigerator that belonged to us. My mother-in-law was keeping it in her basement, plugged in, so it would be usable if we ever needed it again. We told them it wasn't frost-free, like she had wanted, but that they could have it free of charge. They happily accepted our offer and quickly arranged for someone to get it for them.

The minister's wife told us later that when they plugged in the refrigerator at their house, they heard lots of knocking noises coming from it. From that day on, it was a frost-free refrigerator! When we had it in our house, the frost would build up several inches thick, due to my procrastinating about defrosting it!

She told us several years later that it was still frost-free and she had *never* had to defrost it at all! We all agreed that the angels must have been in there working on it to make it frost-free when they first plugged it in at their house. This precious couple had served God faithfully in the ministry for many years, delighting themselves in the Lord continually, and God gave them the desire of their heart. What an awesome God we serve!

> "Delight thyself also in the Lord; and he shall give thee the desires of thine heart" (Psalm 37:4).

CHAPTER TEN

GOD'S LITTLE MESSENGER

When Chris, our second son, was only 18 months old, God used him to carry a message of encouragement to a pastor who was going through a difficult valley, perplexed as to the direction he should take in his ministry. That pastor happened to be his daddy, who was sitting in a chair in the living room, looking very sad.

Chris enjoyed pulling books out of our bookcase, while I was busy in the kitchen or talking on the telephone. This particular day, I was cooking supper and did not realize that Chris was busy pulling more books out of the bookcase. But this time, it was different. He toddled into the living room, holding an opened devotion book in his hand, and handed it to his daddy. My husband began to read the words on the page which said, "It is very easy to fall into the habit of doubting, fretting, and wondering if God has forsaken us and if, after all, our hopes are to end in failure. Let us refuse to be discouraged. Let us refuse to be unhappy. Let us 'count it all joy' when we cannot feel one emotion of happiness . . . . The devil has two master tricks. One is to get us discouraged; then for a time at least we can be of no service to others, and so are defeated. The other is to make us doubt, thus breaking the faith link by which we are bound to our Father. Look out! Do not be tricked either way."[4]

After reading this wonderful message from the devotion book, *Streams in the Desert,* my husband came to the kitchen to ask if I had

---

[4]   Cowman, Mrs. Charles E., *Streams in the Desert,* (Cowman Publishing Company, Inc. 1963), p. 300.

opened the book and prompted Chris to bring it to him. I assured him that our baby had done it on his own. Then I took the book and read the message. We then hugged and rejoiced together knowing that God cared enough about us and our perplexing circumstances to show our little son where to open the book to this glorious message, reminding his daddy of God's love and power. Isn't God wonderful?

> "O magnify the Lord with me, and let us exalt his name together" (Psalm 34:3).

Chapter Eleven

A BOX OF RAISINS

At one point in our ministry, we found ourselves "in between" churches. We had been appointed to a church in another state and had said our goodbyes at the church we were pastoring near Atlanta. We packed all our belongings and drove to our new church, but after arriving there, we were overwhelmed by what we saw there. Everything was totally different from what we were used to, and to be truthful, we just couldn't bear to be so far away from home. After apologizing to the people there, and calling our State Overseer, we drove back to the Atlanta area the next day. We had no home, no jobs, and no church. We had one child in school (Steve) and one toddler (Chris), so we were really in a bad situation.

After staying with my husband's family for 2 or 3 days, we found an apartment to rent until we were assigned to another church. The only money coming in was a small amount each week from another source and the love offerings from churches where Larry would preach on weekends in the Atlanta area. I applied for a job as a substitute teacher to help out with the finances, but I never got a call to teach.

During this period of time, I began to feel that we had really displeased God by not staying at the church in the other state. I even started feeling that God had forsaken us. I remember lying in the living room floor one day, moaning and crying out to God to help us and show us what to do. We both wanted desperately to please God and to be in His will. Although we ministered in different churches on Sundays, we were constantly praying for an open door to pastor again.

A short time after Christmas, when we had been in the apartment for about a month, I was standing in the kitchen and began to think about what I would fix for supper and how I would really like to have some apple salad, like I used to make. We had some apples left over from Christmas, and we had some pecans, cherries, and a jar of mayonnaise, but we didn't have raisins. We were short on money so I didn't go and buy raisins. I don't remember praying about it, I just remember wishing that I had all the ingredients to make an apple salad.

A few days later, my mother-in-law walked in to our apartment and joined us in the kitchen. Before she sat down, she said, "I went to the store today and I don't know why I bought these raisins, but here, you can have them." Then, to my amazement, she promptly put a big box of raisins on our kitchen table!

I knew instantly that God was showing me He had not forsaken us and that He still loved us. I was so thrilled and astounded that He had taken notice of a small desire of mine that nobody else knew about! It was His way of assuring us that He would take care of us and supply our every need.

With uplifted hearts, we made it through a few more weeks and finally received word that we would be going to pastor a church in Savannah, Georgia. Praise God for His unfailing love and for the comfort and care He gives to His children!

> "Behold, I am the Lord, the God of all flesh: is there any
> thing too hard for me?" (Jeremiah 32:27).

CHAPTER TWELVE

GOD MET OUR NEED

While pastoring a church in Savannah, Georgia, there was one Sunday when my husband's paycheck was a total of $42.00. There were four in our family at the time, and we were concerned about how we would buy groceries and other necessities that week.

Larry went to the church to pray about our financial situation. While he was praying at the church, a man came to our parsonage door asking to see the pastor. This man's family attended our church, but he only came occasionally. I walked with him over to the church (which was next door) and interrupted Larry's prayer time to tell him that someone wanted to see him. I left them alone to talk.

When Larry got back to the house, he told me that the man had handed him $60.00! This man was in the tree-cutting business and he had cut down some trees. He said he had told his boss that he was going to give the preacher every penny he made on that job. Larry asked him if he wanted the money to go for the church, and he said, "No." It was for him personally. He then told him that any time he paid tithes on his business, the Lord blessed him with more work than he could handle. We were so thankful and astonished once again to see how God heard and answered prayer while the prayer was still being uttered!

". . . . for your Father knoweth what things ye have need of, before ye ask him" (Matthew 6:8b).

Chapter Thirteen

OTHER EXPERIENCES IN SAVANNAH

In Savannah, Georgia, during the late 1970's, a financial problem came up at the church where we pastored. There was not enough money coming in to pay the church's bills, and something had to be done.

After fasting for several days about the problem, we were amazed to hear that the Lord had been dealing with an elderly gentleman in our church, and gave him the solution to the problem around midnight one night. He said he couldn't sleep that night, and that God spoke to his heart about helping the church. He felt led to propose an offer to loan the church a certain amount of money and let the church pay him back in small payments for a certain amount of time. The men of the church gladly accepted his offer, and this arrangement helped the church so much. Praise God for speaking to this gentleman that night, and for his obedience to the Lord!

I want to mention another thing that happened while we were at that church. We had prayer meetings one night each week in the church sanctuary. We called it the "Hour of Power." At one of our prayer meetings, we only had a few people there to pray. We spread out all over the church sanctuary, kneeling between the church pews. During the prayer meeting, it sounded like a great big group of people had come into the church and were praying loudly. After the prayer meeting ended, I mentioned what I had heard, and others said they heard it too (including my husband). No one else was in the sanctuary, so we all agreed that God must have sent angels that night to our prayer meeting to help us pray! This was an encouragement to those who attended the prayer meeting that night. We believe that God does send reinforcements when needed!

".... make known his deeds among the people"
(I Chronicles 16:8b)

Chapter Fourteen

THE MISSING KEYS

There were two different times when I lost my keys, and I was amazed at how the Lord helped me to find them.

The first time, we were in Marietta, Georgia, and we were living in our own home. I had come into the house after going somewhere in the car, and when I needed to go somewhere else, I could not find my keys anywhere. I searched the house over and over, but still could not find them. In desperation, I got down on the floor on my face in one of the bedrooms and cried out to God for help. After praying, I got up and walked into the bathroom across the hall, and walked straight to the window, where my keys were lying on the window sill!

The second time I lost my keys was while we were living in Savannah, Georgia. We had gone to a Homecoming at one of the churches in our district, on a Sunday afternoon. During the service, our two-year old son, Chris, became restless, so I pulled the keys from my purse and let him play with them.

It wasn't until days later that I realized I had lost my keys. I remembered taking them out at the church, so we called the pastor. He searched for them and could not find them. I searched the house and searched my purse, but I still could not find them. Weeks passed and I became desperate. Once again, I got down on the floor in one of the bedrooms, crying out to God for help. After praying, I felt led to go over to the closet in that room. I opened the door and put my hand in one of the pockets of a little leisure suit that belonged to Chris. THE KEYS WERE IN THAT POCKET! He had been wearing that suit on the day of the Homecoming. I was shocked, just as I was the first time, at how God led me straight to the keys when I had called out to Him desperately for help. Thank God for His awesome power!

". . . . and the thing that is hid bringeth he forth to light"
(Job 28:11).

Chapter Fifteen

THE HIGH CHURCH STEPS

The Lord once showed my father-in-law, F. W. Hemphill, something about our future. We were pastoring in Savannah, Georgia, and we were feeling that it was time to move somewhere else. We were praying about where we should go, and our parents were praying with us about it.

My husband's dad became very ill and while in the hospital, he went into a coma for a few days. But thankfully, he recovered and was sent home. He later told us not to worry—that the Lord had shown him while he was in the hospital that we would be going to another church. He said it would have high (or steep) steps in the front just like the Sharon Baptist church in Smyrna, Georgia. We had seen that church many times before when we lived in Smyrna, so we knew what it looked like.

A short time later, we accepted a pastorate at the Shannon Church of God in Shannon, Georgia (near Rome). We had never been to that town, and had never seen the church until moving day. Our truck pulled up in front of the church, and THERE WERE THE HIGH FRONT STEPS! It was also a red brick church—like the church he had mentioned to us earlier. We knew when we saw it that we were in the right place. I'm sure he was amazed (as we were) about the Lord showing him in advance what our next church would look like. Larry's dad was able to come for only one service at that church, and he walked up those high steps when he came to visit us in the summer. But, sadly, he passed away the following November (in 1977).

> ". . . . marvelous are thy works; and that my soul knoweth right well" (Psalm 139:14b).

CHAPTER SIXTEEN

A REVELATION THROUGH A DREAM

While living in Savannah, Georgia, and praying about what church we would go to next to pastor, I had a dream about a minister in North Georgia whom Larry and I both knew. In the dream, he told us that we would be going to North Rome. This was puzzling to us because the North Rome Church of God in Rome, Georgia, was a much bigger church than ours, and we knew that we couldn't possibly go there. But soon after that, we were sent to the Shannon Church of God in Shannon, Georgia, which was on the *North Rome* District. And who do you think was the youth director for our district? It was the minister I had seen in my dream!

While pastoring at Shannon, Larry was close enough to travel back and forth to Cleveland, Tennessee, to get his Master's degree in Religion at the Church of God School of Theology. He graduated in 1980. I believe that was one purpose the Lord had in mind for us when He sent us to Shannon.

> ". . . . and he that revealeth secrets maketh known to thee what shall come to pass" (Daniel 2:29).

Chapter Seventeen

A LITTLE GIRL HEALED OF A BRAIN TUMOR

In the late 1970's, while pastoring in Shannon, Georgia, we received a phone call from a lady who asked us to come to her house and have prayer for her little granddaughter who had a brain tumor. We had never met this person, but she gave us directions to her house and we went to pray for the little girl, assuming that she was at the house. As it turned out, her granddaughter was not there at her house, but we prayed earnestly and believed God with this precious grandmother for the healing of the brain tumor. I believe this woman was full of faith and confidence in God. It was not a sensational prayer or an extra long prayer, but it was a sincere prayer, and God heard and answered.

The child's grandmother called us later to tell us that when the doctors checked her granddaughter again for the brain tumor, it was gone! Needless to say, we rejoiced with her that day on the phone, happy in knowing that God can do anything!

> ". . . . With men this is impossible; but with God all things
> are possible" (Matthew 19:26).

Chapter Eighteen

HOT TEA

While pastoring at Shannon, Georgia, I dreamed about being in a different place that I didn't recognize, sitting at a table with ladies that I didn't know. While we were sitting there, another lady came up to a window and talked to us through the window from the outside. She was an older lady with a heavy foreign accent and she was wearing a white bonnet, like Dutch women would wear along with their wooden shoes and white aprons. Then someone served me some tea without ice.

We accepted a church in Sarasota, Florida, a short while later. This would be our first time to pastor a church outside of Georgia. My parents told me that my great aunt and uncle lived in Sarasota, but I couldn't remember ever meeting them.

After we had been in Sarasota for a few months, we decided to visit my great aunt and uncle who lived across town. Uncle Arthur greeted us happily at the door, and I remember being amazed to see how much he resembled by mother's brother, Doile King. He then introduced us to his wife, Willie. They welcomed us in and we talked a while. Then Aunt Willie went into the kitchen, and a few minutes later she returned to the living room and served us some hot tea. I noticed that Aunt Willie talked with a heavy foreign accent. She was from the Netherlands and they had met and married while Uncle Arthur was stationed there during the time of his military service years ago.

They visited our church once for a Homecoming Day celebration and Aunt Willie also came to a Mother-Daughter banquet at the church, where she talked with our church ladies in her heavy foreign accent.

I didn't realize until later that my dream had been about Aunt Willie and the ladies at that church. She was a visitor from outside the church, so I suppose that is why I dreamed that she was outside and separate from the other ladies. The hot tea, her foreign accent, the fact that she was an older lady, and the hints about her nationality were all in the dream!

I stand in awe of such a wonderful God who can show us things before they ever happen!

"Be still, and know that I am God . . . ." (Psalm 46:10).

Chapter Nineteen

A FLASH OF LIGHT

While we were living in Sarasota, Florida, we received word that Larry's mother was in the hospital in Marietta, Georgia.

Around that same time, we heard that the State Overseer of Georgia was dying of cancer and needed prayer. So, I felt that I should fast for both of them all the next day, which was a Saturday. I had a very hard time fasting that day. I craved food more than usual, and I had an unusually bad headache. I was tempted to give up and eat so the headache would go away, but I didn't give in to the temptation. I spent extra time in prayer that day, feeling burdened for my mother-in-law and for the minister in Georgia. As soon as I laid my head on my pillow that night, I saw (and felt) a flash of light, like a lightning bolt, come through my head. In a split second the Lord let me know that my prayers had been heard.

The next day, we called to check on my mother-in-law, and she told us that she was better and that she was going home from the hospital. She said that she had seen a red glow around her bed and that an angel came and sat on her bed! I was so amazed when she told us that!

I can't explain the way I felt when the flash of light came through my head, but it was a wonderful feeling that I will never forget. I have since read that light is the emblem of knowledge and that light also means manifestation. I was astounded when I read those words, because I knew that a flash of light was what the Lord had used to show me that my prayer had been answered.

We are in a conflict or warfare with Satan when we fast and pray, so don't ever give in to the temptation to stop fasting or praying when you have felt led of the Lord to do it for a special need. God will give victory if you will hold on!

> "For we wrestle not against flesh and blood, but against principalities, against powers, against the rulers of the darkness of this world, against spiritual wickedness in high places" (Ephesians 6:12).

CHAPTER TWENTY

PASSING A BABY AROUND

While we were living at Shannon, Georgia, I dreamed that I was in a little flat building with lots of ladies, and I was passing a baby around to different ladies in the room. I did not recognize any of the ladies, and did not know whose baby it was that was being passed around for everyone to hold. I felt like I was in a store building or something like that, and that it was built close to the ground.

A short time later, we moved from our church at Shannon to pastor the South Sarasota Church of God in Florida. Our fellowship hall at the church was adjoining the sanctuary and Sunday School rooms, and it had a flat roof on it. It was built close to the ground.

Two years passed, and one night I sat in the fellowship hall surrounded by ladies from our church and we were passing a baby around, my own new baby! It was our third child, Scott! We had hoped and prayed for another baby for several years. The funny thing about it is that I did not realize at the time that my dream had come true. While it was happening it did not occur to me that this was the fulfillment of my dream from two years back. It was not until later that I thought about what had happened and felt stunned and amazed to think that God had shown me a glimpse of what would happen in Sarasota two years before it came to pass!

As I mentioned previously, we had hoped and prayed for another baby for several years. A gynecologist in Rome, Georgia, had advised me to have a hysterectomy and said that I would probably never be able to have another baby due to fibroid tumors. I told him that I would not give up hope. We just kept believing and praying for another child and would not believe the doctor's report.

After moving to Sarasota, I asked the ladies at our Tuesday morning prayer meeting to anoint me and pray for me. I felt a wonderful touch from the Lord that day, and I believe it was then that God heard our prayer about a baby.

A short time later, we were thrilled by the news from my new doctor that we were going to have another baby! The Lord helped me through the pregnancy and on January 2, 1983, Scott was born. He weighed 9 pounds and 13 & 1/2 ounces. He brought a lot of joy and happiness to our home, and needless to say, his brothers adored him.

I sent a letter of witness and a birth announcement to the gynecologist who had said that I would probably never be able to have another baby. I wanted to give God the glory and show the doctor that God still answers prayer.

As I write this, Scott is thirty years old. He has preached at different churches, even while he was still in high school. In college, he majored in Music, specifically Piano Performance. He is a great pianist, and although he can play complicated classical music, we still love to hear him play (and sing) gospel music—Pentecostal style!

If you have been given a seemingly hopeless diagnosis from a doctor, keep holding on to God for a miracle. With God, nothing is impossible!

> "I will remember the works of the Lord: surely I will remember thy wonders of old. I will meditate also of all thy work, and talk of thy doings". "Thou art the God that doest wonders: thou hast declared thy strength among the people" (Psalm 77:11, 12, & 14).

CHAPTER TWENTY ONE

MY DREAM ABOUT A GOLD RING

When we were in our fourth year of pastoring the South Sarasota church in Sarasota, Florida, we began to feel that it was time to go elsewhere. So, we started praying and seeking God for direction. Then one night I had a dream about a gold ring. It had something to do with a little boy being lost. A policeman showed me a gold ring, similar to a senior class ring.

Two days later, a pastor called us from Ringgold, Georgia. He said that the State Overseer of Georgia had told him to call us about exchanging churches (we would go to his church and he would be sent to ours). We talked to him and started praying about it.

Also, I felt led one day to stop what I was doing and read a certain chapter in the Bible (James, chapter 2). The Lord somehow impressed on my mind what to read. Verse 2 was about a man giving a gold ring to his son. I had never realized that this chapter had anything in it about a gold ring.

Another day, I picked up my devotion book and read the March 13th devotion in the book *Streams in the Desert*. It mentioned leaves of gold and a tree with ring after ring of knotty growth.

After much prayer, we finally decided to go to Ringgold, Georgia, and the Lord gave us even more confirmation of our call to go there one Sunday morning during an ordinary service, just before we left our church in Florida. The choir director led the choir in singing "When They Ring Those Golden Bells." Then the soloist sang "City of Gold" and when I asked my friend what she wanted to sing for our duet, she suggested "Someday I'll Walk On Gold," so we sang that! All this was in one service. I was so surprised that all three of those songs mentioned "gold" or "ring."

We did move to Ringgold, Georgia, shortly after that, and we stayed a little over four years there. For two and a half years of that time, I had the opportunity of writing a weekly devotional article in the local newspaper, *The Catoosa County News*. It was an open door to minister to thousands of people in and around our community that may not have been reached with the gospel any other way.

Living at Ringgold also made a wonderful difference in the life of our middle son, Chris. He took drum lessons from an expert drummer while we were there, and this brightened up his life. This drum teacher had played with the Chattanooga Symphony Orchestra and the U. S. Marine Band. Chris really looked up to him and practiced a lot so that he could play the drums as well as his teacher. Taking drum lessons helped him to gain self-confidence. I would practice with him at home on the piano or organ, and he started playing drums at church (really well) in just a short period of time. He still enjoys playing drums, and he sings, also. Over the last few years, he has preached in different churches and has been used of God to pray the prayer of faith for the sick. He also served as youth pastor at his church. The Lord knows what He is doing when He sends us to a particular place. He always knows best!

> "I will mention the lovingkindnesses of the Lord, and the praises of the Lord, according to all that the Lord hath bestowed on us . . . ." (Isaiah 63:7a).

Chapter Twenty Two

THE TOMATO TREE

While pastoring at Ringgold, Georgia, we were praying about going elswhere after being there for almost four years. Our plans were to go back to Florida. All summer, we thought we would probably move to Lacoochee, Florida. The church there had been mentioned to us. We made a trip down there to see the church and parsonage, but we could not decide for sure if it was where we should go at that time.

One night, I had an unusual dream. I saw an orange tree, and while I was staring at it, the oranges changed to tomatoes. I thought that was so strange!

As it turned out, our plans changed and we later went to Cornelius, North Carolina, to pastor a church there. As we drove into the town for the first time, we saw a white frame house with a big banner stretched across the front porch, which read "TOMATOES." Then I realized the dream meant that instead of going to Florida, where there were orange trees, we would be going to Cornelius, where people often sold tomatoes on the main street of town. The church people also brought us tomatoes while we were there.

After we had pastored Cornelius for two years, we THEN went to Lacoochee, Florida, to pastor there.

> "Trust in the Lord with all thine heart; and lean not unto
> thine own understanding. In all thy ways acknowledge
> him, and he shall direct thy paths" (Proverbs 3: 5&6).

CHAPTER TWENTY THREE

PROTECTION DURING A HURRICANE

It was August of 1989 when we accepted the pastorate at the Cornelius Church of God in Cornelius, North Carolina. This town is located a few miles north of Charlotte. We had only been there about a month and a half when hurricane Hugo hit our area. It was expected to pound the coast of South Carolina, near Charleston, and then move on up the coast. But instead, it came inland with great force and went all the way to Charlotte and beyond. No one was prepared for the horrible winds, rain, and tornadoes that came through our area.

Our family had attended an area-wide church service in Charlotte on Thursday night, just before the hurricane was expected to hit Charleston. It was slightly windy and raining just a little, but it did not bother us in the least, since we thought the hurricane was headed only for the coast. We had been warned of possible flooding due to the heavy rain, but that was all that the weather forecasters had mentioned.

We returned home that night and went to bed with no idea of what was headed in our direction. We woke up a few hours later, due to the powerful winds. It sounded like one freight train after another going up and down our street. This lasted for hours.

The two things that concerned me were the town water tower, located just behind our back yard, and the huge tree at the end of our back yard. I feared that if the wind blew either one of these over on our house, we would all die. I remember Larry saying, "Go back to sleep. It's not as bad as it sounds." But instead, I laid awake the rest of the night (in between peeks out of our bedroom window), praying desperately for God's protection and help. Larry woke up and started praying too as the storm got worse. Around 5:00 A.M. the noise was so terrifying, we both got up. We turned on the television to see what was happening, but the electricity went off shortly after that.

What a shock when daybreak came and we could see the damage that was done to our neighborhood! Our next door neighbor came to our door to tell us about some of the damage.

There were leaves and tree twigs all over our yard. Trees were lying across roads all over town, and a big tree had fallen into the front of our neighbor's house, just two houses up from us. Thankfully, no one was in that house. Many houses were damaged and the huge oak trees on the campus of nearby Davidson College were completely uprooted. Charlotte was hit hard with damage all over the city. Many people had fled to Charlotte for refuge, but to no avail.

But the miracle I want to tell you about is this: Our garbage cans, which would normally blow over with a slight puff of wind, were still standing upright in their place. Also, we had some empty pasteboard boxes that Larry had placed on top of our garbage cans in the backyard, and they did not blow away, even though tornado-like winds blew all around our house. The light-weight and fragile utility house in our back yard was still standing, undamaged, and our house was not damaged at all.

Our phone was out of order from Thursday night until Saturday afternoon, so we couldn't call our parents and they couldn't call us during that time. (This was before cell phones!) We did have water at our house, although others in the area did not. Our electricity was off until Sunday. We decided to have church Sunday night by using oil lamps and candles, but to our surprise, the lights came on just as we opened the doors of the church!

When Larry was finally able to call his mother to let her know we were all right, she said she wasn't worried. She said that the Lord had spoken to her heart and said, "I sent him there—don't you think I can take care of him?"

We will always be grateful for God's protecting power over us and our two youngest children, Chris and Scott, who were with us in the house. He protected our house, our car, and everything in our yard, as well as our church. Yes, we will always remember hurricane Hugo, but we will also remember how God watched over us through that terrifying night!

> ". . . . What manner of man is this, that even the winds
> and the sea obey him?" (Matthew 8:27b).

Rev. Larry and Diane Hemphill

(Left to right)—Scott, Chris, Larry, and Steve

Diane and Larry with their children and grandchildren

Steve, Adrianna, and Mateo

Chris & Crystal

Scott and Whitney with their children, Lily, Locke, and
Levi (in front)

Diane with her parents, Rachel and Charles Moss

Diane with her mother, Rachel; her brother, David, and
her sister, Brenda (on the right)

Larry's parents, Geneva and Fulton W. Hemphill

Larry with his brothers and sisters: (left to right)—Jane,
Larry, Tommy, Richard, and Mary Grace

Diane and Larry

Diane's brother, Jerry Moss (1949-1973)

CHAPTER TWENTY FOUR

TWO LADIES WHO PRAYED

When our youngest son, Scott, was six years old and in the first grade, he had his first kidney stone. He suffered many days and nights with horrible pain due to the stone. This was in December of 1989, while we were pastoring the Cornelius Church of God at Cornelius, North Carolina. The doctor was giving him medication and allowing him some time to pass the stone before doing a second IV test. Of course, we were praying and our church people were praying for him, but two elderly ladies from our church felt led to give themselves to prayer all day on the day before the IV was to be done. Sister Barnhardt and Sister Kerley were the ladies who prayed that day. They were faithful ladies who knew how to touch God.

That very afternoon, around five o'clock, Scott passed the stone! The doctor was amazed at the size of it. Only God could have worked a miracle like that for Scott, and we praised Him for hearing and answering prayer. We were so grateful to those two ladies who cared enough to pray all day for our son. They have since gone on to be with the Lord, and I know the Lord will reward them for their loving concern and their faithfulness to pray.

"God is our refuge and strength, a very present help in trouble" (Psalm 46:1).

CHAPTER TWENTY FIVE

WATCH YOUR STEP!

I once saw a vision that kept my husband and me from making the wrong move to another location. We were pastoring at Cornelius, North Carolina, and we were praying about whether or not we should go to pastor a certain church not too far from where we lived. The State Overseer of North Carolina had mentioned to us that this particular church might be available soon. Later, Larry talked with the pastor there about the possibility of our going there when he left. So, we began to seek the Lord about His will and what He wanted us to do.

Then one morning as I was just waking up, I saw a short vision. All I saw was the pants legs and shoes of two men on some steps, and I heard the words, "Watch Your Step!" We knew immediately that the Lord was warning us not to go to that particular church, and we did not go. It was such a clear answer from the Lord, and we were thankful that He showed us in such a definite way that we should stay where we were.

We stayed on at our church a while longer and the church people worked with us in a wonderful way. We were able to make improvements on the fellowship hall and then we remodeled the whole church within just 3 or 4 months' time. Also, Larry felt led to ask one of the ladies at the church if she would lead our children's church on Sunday mornings. She said the Lord had already been dealing with her about it. She had lots of puppets and was good at working with children. The children's church ministry grew tremendously under her direction.

Praise the Lord for His warnings to stay where we were, as well as His guidance in handling matters to help the church go forward. He will always guide us if we will just seek His face.

> "And my tongue shall speak of thy righteousness and of thy praise all the day long" (Psalm 35:28).

Chapter Twenty Six

THE WRONG SIDE OF FLORIDA

While we were still pastoring in Cornelius, North Carolina, Larry had two puzzling dreams. In the first dream, he was at the Georgia Church of God campground. His younger sister, Mary Grace, came up to talk to him. He told her that we were going to be moving to Florida to the Bay Church of God and he told her that he wasn't sure of the location of the church yet. Then she gave him sad news. She told him that their mother had passed away.

The second dream started out with him going into a room and getting a letter out of an open mailbox. The letter was from a State Overseer telling him that he would be going to Florida. After he had opened the letter and read the message, all of a sudden he felt that he was looking down (maybe from an airplane) on an aerial view of the state of Florida. A certain section of the state caught his attention, and it was a long county on the Atlantic coast. When Larry saw this, he thought, "That's on the wrong side of Florida!" He felt this way because his thoughts were that we would be going to the Gulf side (as we had twice before) and not on the Atlantic side.

After he finished reading the letter, he heard his dad (who had passed away previously), calling out to his mother, crying "Gene!" Then he saw his mother and she said that she was going to be with his dad. He woke up crying and was terribly upset about the dream.

I am sad to say, Larry's mother did pass away while we were still living at Cornelius, North Carolina. She died in March of 1991. But it was two years later before we were sent to that "long county on the wrong side of Florida," which turned out to be Brevard County. We moved there in 1993 to pastor the North Melbourne Church of God, which was located in the greater Melbourne-Palm Bay area. It wasn't until years later that we realized what the word Bay meant! We had church members who lived in Palm Bay, we went to doctors in Palm Bay, and went to eat at restaurants often in Palm Bay.

Everything happened in the order that it was revealed. First, Larry's mother passed away, and later we were sent to Melbourne, Florida, on the wrong side of the state!

It is so astonishing to us how God has revealed to us certain words, objects, and even places, years before we would actually go there to minister. He is such a mighty God!

> "Behold, the former things are come to pass, and new
> things do I declare: before they spring forth I tell you of
> them" (Isaiah 42:9).

CHAPTER TWENTY SEVEN

THE TWO "AUDITORIUMS"

In 1991, while still living in Cornelius, North Carolina and pastoring the Cornelius Church of God, I dreamed that we went to another church to pastor. I thought it was our first Sunday at the new church. I didn't see the outside of the church. As the dream began, we were standing inside the vestibule next to a table that was covered with a cloth, sort of like a sheet or a tablecloth. A young man who looked like an Indian was standing there by the table.

We started into the sanctuary or auditorium in front of us, but someone directed us to go in a different direction to "the other auditorium." So we went into a very large room and were greeted by some more of the church people. The dream ended, and I did not think much about it at the time.

Around that time, we were feeling that it was time to go to another church, but we didn't know where. Again, we prayed and the Lacoochee Church of God in Florida became available. Soon after that, our State Overseer gave his approval of our going there. The church voted for us to come, so we felt that it was God's will.

As it turned out, the vestibule in the front of the church had a table completely covered with a long cloth. There was a young man who came to the church during our first few months there, and he had dark skin and dark hair. He looked like he might be part Indian. He was the grandson of an elderly couple from the church.

When we moved there, the church had been in a building project for about seven years, serving dinners (as a fund-raiser) every other

Friday in their tiny kitchen and adjoining Sunday School rooms. They were building a new fellowship hall that was connected to the back of the sanctuary. It was huge! We helped to paint it on the inside, scrape windows, clean floors and ceiling fans, and things like that. I helped cook for the workers who would come almost every day, and then cooked every other Friday for the dinners. When the fellowship hall was almost finished, we were able to have the fund-raising dinners in it every other week, feeding big crowds of people who would come from all around to eat the delicious meals that our ladies (and men) had prepared. We served them on nice plates and in a serving line (cafeteria style). There was no charge for the dinners, just a suggested donation of $4.00. Many people gave more than that, and we were able to make from $500 to $1000 at each dinner.

We had programs and parties in the new fellowship hall, but most important of all—it was used as an auditorium on Dedication Day. We had a special service and a dinner that day, and we presented plaques to honor those who had helped with the building project. The fellowship hall was also used as an auditorium when the children presented a special play for the church.

I might add that by Dedication Day, the debt for the building of the fellowship hall was completely paid. It was a joy to see the project completed while we were there, and to be a part in helping to get it finished. It was beautiful! It had a pastor's study in the back, a big storage room for chairs and tables, two restrooms, and of course, a nice kitchen. We enjoyed many activities in that huge "auditorium," made possible by the hard-working people at the church and by a group called the Mappers, who assisted with the work toward the end of the project.

God really helped us and gave us strength to do the work that was necessary during our pastorate at Lacoochee. We made many friends and we will always remember them. We had good music and singing there, also. We trust that our ministry there was a blessing.

"For this God is our God for ever and ever: he will be our
guide even unto death" (Psalm 48:14).

CHAPTER TWENTY EIGHT

LARRY'S DREAM ABOUT A BLACK SNAKE

While we were living in Lacoochee, Florida, Larry had a dream about seeing a black snake in the back yard. In the dream, he got a shovel and tried to kill it, but missed it. Then the snake started chasing him. He woke up at that time and thought about the dream.

The very next day, he was in the back yard and saw a black snake that was identical to the one he had seen in his dream. So, instead of trying to kill it as he normally might have done, he slowly backed away from it and went into the house. Larry said he knew for sure that God gave him the dream to warn him not to bother the snake and to just leave it alone. Thank God for the warning ahead of time that protected him from danger!

"For he shall give his angels charge over thee, to keep thee in all thy ways" (Psalm 91:11).

CHAPTER TWENTY NINE

THE CHURCH NEAR A STATE LINE

After pastoring the Lacoochee Church of God in Florida for a while, we began to seek the Lord about where He would have us to go from there. Larry contacted the State Overseer of Georgia about going back to that state. After a while, he gave us the name of a pastor who might be interested in coming to our church. If so, we would be sent to his church. He was the pastor of the Trenton Church of God in North Georgia, near the border of Georgia, Alabama, and Tennessee.

I had already experienced a dream about living in a house close to a state line, but I didn't know which state line. As it turned out, the Alabama state line was very close by. Larry contacted the pastor there, and they talked about our church and parsonage, as well as his. He mentioned that there was an arch or archway between the living room and kitchen. Larry told me about the arch. Then later that day, I opened my Bible where my marker was, to read the next three chapters, as I do each day. It was Ezekiel, chapter 40, and the word "arches" was mentioned 15 times! I underlined it every time I came to it. I could not believe it!

Later, I had several dreams about a church and parsonage, but I didn't know where I was in the dream. I dreamed that I saw people walking down a stairway that went sideways and then straight down. I thought that Larry had to go upstairs to turn on the furnace. I picked up toys off the floor in a Sunday School room upstairs. At one point in the dream, I could hear children singing from another place in the church. I saw myself sitting at an old table in an old-looking Sunday

School room. My thoughts were that the church didn't look so good on the inside, but at least our house was nice.

We did move to the Trenton church a few weeks later. After we had been there a while, I realized that those dreams were of the Trenton Church of God. You see, Larry had to go upstairs to turn on the furnace. I realized one day that I had straightened up an upstairs Sunday School room, picking toys up off the floor, just like it was in the dream. Every Sunday, I saw our church people walking up and down those stairs that went sideways and then straight down. Also, we could hear the children singing at times, from their children's church room, located on the level beneath the sanctuary. I taught Sunday School in classrooms that looked old and had old tables in them.

In one dream that I had before we ever moved to Trenton, I was looking at a street that was level at the beginning and then went uphill. I saw a small house on the right side and then a hill beyond that. There were flowers all around the neighborhood. I remember looking for the church and it was not anywhere to be found on that street.

On moving day, when we actually drove into Trenton to find the parsonage, it was situated exactly as I had seen it in my dream, on the right side of the street, on the part just before the hill. It was a small house. There were pretty flowers blooming in our yard, and in the neighbors' yards. The church was located several blocks away, not on the same street as the parsonage.

In one of my dreams, I saw ladies in the church with old fashioned hairstyles, and I saw children rejoicing around the altar. Some of our church ladies did wear their hair up in old fashioned hairstyles, and Scott (our 10 year old son) received the Holy Ghost in the altar while praising the Lord in a good service.

While still in Florida, before we ever got word that we would be moving, I looked up in the sky after we had visited a lady in the University Hospital in Tampa. There was a perfect cross, formed by clouds in the sky, and it stayed there for a few minutes and then vanished. It was very unusual. My thoughts were: "Is the Lord showing me that we are going to pastor a church called Crossroads or Church of the Cross, or maybe Calvary Church of God?" It wasn't until much later that I realized what the cross made of clouds was all about. There were three crosses on the wall behind the choir at the Trenton church, and we could see them every time we looked toward the choir or pulpit.

The Lord did help us while we were there, and we were blessed with a wonderful group of people. It was a great town in which to live. I took some more piano lessons there, Scott played on a baseball team, and we felt relaxed enough to go walking several evenings each week at the recreation area nearby.

God's purpose for our going there, we believe, was so that we could be near Chris during his first year at Lee University. We did not go there for this purpose, but as it turned out, he desperately needed our help that year when he became very ill with the flu. We brought him home to take care of him, and it was a comfort to him and to us to live close to each other.

God supplied our every need during our time there, and someday we will be shown the results of our labors while pastoring there.

"Blessed be the Lord God, the God of Israel, who only
doeth wondrous things" (Psalm 72:18).

CHAPTER THIRTY

LEAVE IT ALONE!

In 1993, while we were pastoring the Trenton Church of God in Trenton, Georgia, our financial situation became desperate at one point. We were about to panic, so I decided I would go out and look for a job.

I put my application in at the school, but never heard from them. I also put my application in at a local bank for a job as a teller. I finally got a call from the bank, and they wanted me to come in for an interview. Actually, five different people interviewed me on two separate days. It seemed that they all liked me, so I was pretty certain that I would be hired. I prayed earnestly for the Lord's will to be done. I wanted to continue to be free to help my husband in the ministry, visiting homes and hospitals and things like that. I was terrified of handling money, but I was willing to work there to help with our finances, if that was what the Lord wanted me to do.

After many days had passed and I still had not heard from them, Larry and I were getting impatient and anxious about our financial situation. So I decided to call the bank and ask them if they had made a decision about my coming to work there. But before I went to the kitchen to pick up the phone, I heard the words "LEAVE IT ALONE!" very clearly in my mind. I did not hear an audible voice, just those words distinctly in my mind. I knew then that I had better not call the bank, but I should just leave it alone, instead.

I never heard from the people at the bank, but immediately our church began to do better and our financial situation improved. My God is an awesome God! He knows how to solve every problem.

> "As for me, I will call upon God; and the Lord shall save me" (Psalm 55:16).

CHAPTER THIRTY ONE

A GENEROUS GIFT

After pastoring the Trenton Church of God for a while, we felt that the Lord was leading us to go elsewhere, so we prayed earnestly for months about where we should go. A church in Melbourne, Florida was mentioned to Larry when he talked to the State Overseer of Florida, but several months passed while we waited for a decision to be made by the pastor there.

Meanwhile, the Lord was showing us things and giving us definite signs that we should go to Melbourne, so we kept praying and believing God to work it out, and He did!

As we made plans to move to Melbourne, the pastor there told us that his parsonage in Melbourne was unfurnished. Our parsonage in Trenton was furnished except for one bedroom. He asked if we wanted to buy some of their furniture. He sent us pictures of the furniture so we could see what it looked like. He wanted to sell two queen size beds, a night stand, two dressers, a chest of drawers with a mirror, and a computer desk. He was asking $600 for the furniture. We desperately needed the furniture if we were going to live there, so we sent him a check for $600.

Then, the night before we left Trenton, a precious lady from our church called and asked if she could come by for a moment. She came and would only stand in the doorway. She handed us an envelope, hugged us, and said "goodbye." We thanked her and said a tearful "goodbye." Larry opened the envelope after she left, and it contained a check for $600! This was EXACTLY what we had just paid for the furniture! No one knew that we had bought any furniture or what we had paid for it—except God! How we rejoiced over that! We knew for certain then, that God was sending us to Melbourne and was seeing to it that every obstacle was removed and every need was met so we could go there. What a great God we serve! By the way, we called the lady who brought us the check, thanking her profusely, and we told her later about the miracle God had wrought through her gift.

> "But my God shall supply all your need according to his
> riches in glory by Christ Jesus" (Philippians 4:19).

CHAPTER THIRTY TWO

HORSES AND ARMADILLOS

While pastoring at Trenton, Georgia, and seeking God for direction about where to go next, we were amazed at how the Lord gave us clues about things we would see when we got to the next place.

The most prominent sign (or clue) was horses. First of all, the Lord gave me the word "horse" one day while I was praying in our extra bedroom. Then, someone gave us a Guidepost magazine, and I read a story about horses and dogs. After that, we were absolutely astonished at how many horses we saw. Pictures of horses were in the magazines we opened, on billboards and on television. We even saw a horse and buggy in downtown Trenton.

One day we went to a gift shop where one of our church members worked, and she was showing us some new pictures that had come in. It shocked us when she laid a picture of a horse on the top of the stack for us to see. In restaurants, we would sit down at a table and there would be a picture of a horse on the wall near our table. Things like this went on for months.

I must explain that a pastor from Melbourne, Florida, was thinking about coming to pastor where we were (at Trenton) after our state overseer told him that we might be interested in going to Florida. He couldn't make up his mind about whether to come or not, even after coming to visit us to see our church and our house. But, during a phone conversation one day, Larry asked him if there was anything to do with horses in the Melbourne area. I think he was shocked, because he knew we had never been to Melbourne and knew nothing about the area. He began to tell Larry that there was a big racing track for horses and dogs not far from his church. Also, he said there were horse stables in the neighborhood and at a nearby park. I believe that is when that pastor realized that God must be showing us where to go.

After months of prayer, feeling that we should go to Melbourne, the pastor and his wife finally made the decision to come and pastor the Trenton church where we were, and we went to pastor the North Melbourne church where they were. Of course, both State Overseers approved the change, and also the churches voted before the actual change took place.

On moving day, after driving for many, many hours, we found the street where our new church was located, and started to drive down it. When we rounded a curve, there was a highway sign that read "CAUTION—HORSE AREA". I will never forget the excitement I felt when I saw that highway sign. The Lord had been showing us for months that we would be going to a place where horses were all around. We saw horse stables on that street, and later in a nearby park. The main thing, though, was the huge horse and dog-racing track not far from where we lived. It was incredible!

Also, during the time of seeking the Lord for direction and waiting on the Lord before being sent to North Melbourne, I had a very strange dream about an armadillo. At that time, I had never even seen a real armadillo. But in my dream, I saw an armadillo come into my kitchen. I was afraid of it, and I knew I had to get rid of it somehow. I grabbed some newspapers, picked up the armadillo, and stuffed it into my kitchen trash can. Then I woke up. I told Larry about it later, but I didn't know that the dream would ever have any meaning for us.

Then, shortly after we moved to Melbourne, I went to eat lunch with some of the ladies from our church after our Tuesday morning prayer meeting. While we were riding along, one of the ladies pointed to a nice building and said, "That's where they study about armadillos." I couldn't believe what I was hearing! I knew we were in the right place.

Later, we saw many armadillos on the side of the road, having been hit by cars as they tried to cross the road. How amazing that the Lord would show me an armadillo in a dream—right before we moved to a place where armadillos were a common thing. We had never lived in a place where armadillos were around.

We have many wonderful memories of the people we met and the experiences we had during our two years at the North Melbourne Church of God. We still hear from friends who went to the church there. Melbourne is a beautiful city with palm trees everywhere, and we enjoyed living near the ocean. The Lord blessed our church there with great services and many answers to prayer.

> "Thou wilt shew me the path of life: in thy presence is fulness of joy; at thy right hand there are pleasures for evermore" (Psalm 16:11).

CHAPTER THIRTY THREE

HOW AN EMPTY ROOM WAS FILLED WITH FURNITURE

When we were getting ready to go to pastor in Melbourne, Florida, we knew we would have plenty of bedroom furniture because (as I mentioned previously) we had bought it earlier from the pastor who was leaving there. Unfortunately, he told us that the big living room would be completely empty. We didn't have living room furniture, but we just decided not to worry about it, and planned to put our piano and television in there and maybe a desk and a recliner. Just before we moved, my brother, David, and his wife, Jane, gave us a brown sofa bed to take with us. We were so thankful for that, and we put it in the living room when we got there.

Then, a few months later, some relatives of one of our church families called one day and said they wanted to give us a sofa and chair and a rocking chair. They brought the furniture to the parsonage and we put the sofa and chair in the living room also. It was now filled to capacity!

The rocking chair was immediately put in Scott's bedroom. You see, he was 11 years old at the time, and he had always loved to rock in a rocking chair. He had told us of his desire to have one in his room, so when the Lord sent us the rocking chair, we knew exactly where it should go! The Lord not only supplied our need abundantly, but He gave Scott the desire of his heart. God is so good!

". . . . the goodness of God endureth continually"
(Psalm 52:1b).

Chapter Thirty Four

MY WURLITZER ORGAN

While we were pastoring the North Melbourne Church of God, I finally found the kind of keyboard that I had been looking for. I had hoped for one for several years, but had never found what I liked until we went to a music store on Merritt Island. It was a Yamaha Clavinova, and it was more than what we could afford.

We talked to the salesman there about trading in my Wurlitzer organ and possibly my piano as well, to help lower the price of the keyboard. He gave us a price for trading in the piano and the organ, but the more I thought about giving up my piano, the more upset I became. I really enjoyed having a regular piano and did not want to give it up. I prayed about it before we made a decision, and asked the Lord to show us what to do.

Finally, we told the salesman that we only wanted to trade in the organ, and we asked him how much he would give us for the organ. We were shocked when he quoted a certain amount that was exactly the amount we had paid for the organ fifteen years earlier when it was brand new! Besides this, he still had not seen my organ. It still looked brand new, but he did not know that. So, we bought the beautiful new Clavinova keyboard, and I still had my piano to play.

The story does not end here! A few years later, we went to pastor the Reidsville Church of God. The church had a very old and out-of-tune piano. After a short while, we both felt the Lord leading us to donate our piano to the church. We did so, and the music at the church sounded so much better after that! The church people were thrilled to have a better piano.

Within a few months after donating my piano to the Reidsville church, we received love offerings from the church that far exceeded what we had paid for my piano when we bought it from my sister-in-law many years earlier. Isn't God good?

".... his ways are everlasting" (Habakkuk 3:6b).

CHAPTER THIRTY FIVE

A COMFORTING DREAM

While we were living in Melbourne, Florida, during the mid-1990's, I learned by talking to my mother on the phone, that a sore of some kind had appeared on the back of her head. It was painful and bothersome to her, and she became very concerned over it, especially since it would not go away. I was praying earnestly for her healing, and I was very concerned that it might be a cancerous tumor. You might say I was WORRIED!

One night when I was especially anxious over Mother's condition, I had a dream. I thought I was in Gatlinburg, Tennessee, walking down the busy sidewalk in front of the shops. There were people sitting on benches on both sides of me, and they were singing the chorus, "God Is So Good". They sang:

"God is so good, God is so good,
God is so good, everything's all right."

I thought, "That's not the way it goes! That last line is wrong!" Then I woke up and started thinking about the dream, and realized immediately that those words I had thought were "wrong" were God's message to me that everything was going to be all right with Mother. That dream comforted my heart and gave me sweet peace immediately.

Everything did turn out to be all right. Mother's doctor finally diagnosed the problem and prescribed medicine that helped to heal the sore place completely. I believe the Lord helped it to heal also. I praise God for the way He comforts us and gives us peace in the midst of our storms.

> "Who comforteth us in all our tribulation, that we may
> be able to comfort them which are in any trouble, by the
> comfort wherewith we ourselves are comforted of God"
> (II Corinthians 1:4).

CHAPTER THIRTY SIX

BOOTS, SHEEP, AND DALMATIAN DOGS

Near the end of our two-year stay at the North Melbourne Church of God in Melbourne, Florida, we began to feel that the Lord wanted us to go back to North Carolina. Larry felt that he should contact the pastor at the Hazelwood Church of God near Waynesville, North Carolina, to see if he would be interested in coming back to Florida to pastor. We heard that this man had pastored in Florida in the past, and that the Hazelwood church was a good church. I was against it for a while, because I didn't feel that we should try to open a door on our own, but instead, we should wait for God to open it. But after a while, I began to feel that maybe God was in it after all.

The pastor at Hazelwood seemed interested at first, but then he backed out. We prayed about it and asked the Lord to show us His will. The Lord had already been showing us certain things that we would see at the next place, but we just didn't know where that place would be. He put different things in front of our faces over and over again, until we realized that He was trying to tell us something. Some of the things He showed us were: boots, sheep, and Dalmatian dogs. We would see these things, or pictures of them, almost everywhere we went. We even went to a housewarming party, and one of the gifts given to the family was a kitchen towel with a picture of boots on it! Also, that same family gave us a book about the Church of God in

North Carolina (for no particular reason). Then, they showed us their Dalmatian dog in the back yard.

We knew that God was showing us things we would see at our next church. He had worked this way in our lives so many times before. We kept all these things in mind while waiting on the Lord for direction.

Finally, our State Overseer and the overseer of North Carolina got together and approved the change after the pastor from North Carolina said he indeed wanted to come to our church. The two churches voted (several weeks apart). We were voted in at Hazelwood and then the North Melbourne church voted for that pastor to come there. Much prayer and fasting was done through the whole process, so it wasn't just a decision we made without serious consideration. We sought God's face earnestly for months before all this took place.

We packed up and moved to Hazelwood, North Carolina in August of 1995. Steve, our oldest son, drove our moving truck for us that day. Some of the men at Hazelwood helped us move in, and the church people had prepared supper for us at the church fellowship hall. Larry and Scott went on to the church, while Steve and I finished getting ready. Chris was absent, due to attending college in Tennessee at this time. When Steve drove in to the church parking lot, the first thing I saw was Dalmatian dogs in a fence beside the parking lot! I pointed my finger at them and yelled, "Steve, look—Dalmatian dogs!"

Then, shortly after we moved there, we found out that there was a boot factory near the church that made boots for the soldiers in the Persian Gulf War. It was still in business, and one of our church ladies had even worked there, making boots.

The most amazing part (to me) was that there was a huge picture on the wall behind the pulpit. It was a picture of 6 or 7 sheep grazing in a pasture. I marveled about the Lord showing me the sheep before we ever got there, and I praised Him many times as I looked at the picture during the services. Also, someone had decorated the church bulletin board with pictures of sheep before we arrived there. Why? I don't know, except that God was confirming that we were in the right place.

We stayed at Hazelwood almost two years and enjoyed our time there. We had to cook a lot of church dinners to help pay the bills, but the people worked hard and worked well together. They were good to us and made us feel at home.

Just before we made our announcement that we were leaving the Hazelwood church to go to Reidsville, the Lord gave one of our close friends and church members a dream, showing her that we would be leaving. In her dream, she saw us leaving with a moving truck, and she said she felt sad. She told us about her dream and we were stunned. God does show His people what He is about to do!

> "Lead me, O Lord, in thy righteousness . . . . ; make thy
> way straight before my face" (Psalm 5:8).

CHAPTER THIRTY SEVEN

JONQUILS, CONES, CROWN, AND CORD

We went to pastor the Reidsville Church of God in North Carolina in 1997, after spending about two years at Hazelwood, North Carolina. The pastor at Reidsville was retiring.

Before we knew where we would be going, I dreamed about a house on a hill with a jonquil plant in the front yard. In my dream, Scott and I were standing in the front yard, and I pulled the jonquil plant out of the ground as we talked. As it turned out, there was a jonquil plant in the front yard of the Reidsville parsonage, and it was pulled out of the ground, not by me, but by one of the church members, with our permission, while she was trying to "fix up" our yard. I might add that the parsonage was on a slight hill.

The night before we moved to Reidsville, we were invited to dinner at an elderly couple's house (in Hazelwood). They served the meal at a table on their screened-in front porch. All around the top of the porch (on the inside) were plastic ice cream cones. I had never seen anything like that before, so I took notice of it.

Then, while we were at Reidsville, Scott had some outpatient surgery at Moses Cone Hospital in Greensboro, and we also traveled on Cone Boulevard many times as we went to the mall or other places around Greensboro. It was amazing to me to think about how we had seen those unusual cones the night before we moved!

I had written down several words that I felt the Lord was showing me before we moved to Reidsville. One of the words was "crown." What could that possibly mean? After we had been living in Reidsville for a good while, I finally realized what the word "crown" was all about. One day I looked at the front dealer tag of the car we had bought while living there, and it was a tag from Crown Honda where we had bought the car. That is when I remembered I had written down "crown" as one of my "signs" before moving there.

"Cord" was another word I had written down before we moved. For weeks after we moved, we went all over town looking for a certain kind of cord for Scott's electric drums so he could play drums for the church services. When the Lord first gave me that word, I thought maybe we would be moving to Concord, North Carolina, but it meant something entirely different.

What is really strange is that I also wrote down the words "sea" and "grove" and "Bethel" before moving to Reidsville in 1997. I wrote these words down because the Lord put them in front of my face over and over and over again. Someone had mentioned to us around that time that the Bethel church at Seagrove was a good church, and I even remember thinking that maybe the Lord would send us there someday, but it was never offered to us back then. So, I just dismissed it from my mind. But in December of 2002 (after pastoring two other churches besides Reidsville), the Lord sent us to the Bethel Church of God in Seagrove, North Carolina!

We stayed at Reidsville for a little over two years, and we enjoyed our pastorate there. The people were good to us, and we were always having food and fellowship together in a happy atmosphere. Lasting friendships were made there. Also, this is where we were when we found another great piano teacher for Scott, one who taught him to play church music so beautifully. He took his lessons in Danville, Virginia, from Neal Durham, the Minister of Music at the Riveroaks Church of God. We believe that was one of the reasons we were sent to live at Reidsville. Without this additional music foundation, Scott would never have advanced as far as he has in music. God has a divine plan for us, as well as our children, and it is wonderful to see how He works out His plans!

"For thou art my rock and my fortress; therefore for thy name's sake lead me, and guide me" (Psalm 31:3).

Chapter Thirty Eight

EAGLES, SWANS, AND BICYCLES

During the last year of our pastorate at the Reidsville Church of God, we began to feel that it was time for us to go elsewhere. So, as usual, we began to pray and seek the Lord about where to go. Somehow, the Lord impressed me to write down the word "eagle." I kept seeing the word over and over, and we would see things about eagles on television and other places. The same thing was true about swans and bicycles, so I wrote these words down also and just waited to see what all these words would mean to us in our future.

After advising our State Overseer of our desire to move, we heard from him in the summer of 1999. Without going into all the details, let me just say that everything was worked out for us to go to Bryson City, North Carolina. After going to a Wednesday night service to preach and sing for them, the church voted for us to come as their pastor.

I kept looking for something about eagles there, but couldn't find a thing. But later on, we realized that the county we lived in (Swain County) was shaped like an eagle with its wings spread. They put the shape of it on the county road signs, and you can clearly see on a map of North Carolina that Swain County is shaped like an eagle.

Then, a picture of a swan was on a downtown dress shop window (and on their sign) in Bryson City. We saw it constantly.

As for the bicycle, one of our members (our choir director) was a bicycle enthusiast who rode many miles each day over mountainous terrain. He entered bicycle races for the sheer joy of competition.

How can the Lord show you signs like these ahead of time? He does it by His Spirit, and although it is hard to comprehend, we know He has done it for us many times.

Allow me to tell of one incident that happened in one of our services. We were all praying around the altar at the end of a service. We were in a revival with the Rev. David Maney, a devout man of God who had been a Church of God minister for many years. I had been burdened about something and just could not get it off my mind. While praying about it in the altar, Brother Maney came to me and said, "Sister Hemphill, God says, lay it on the altar." I immediately started crying and rejoicing, and the burden lifted right then!

We enjoyed our two years at Bryson City. We had many good spiritual services, with beautiful singing and music in each service. It was a worshipping church, and you could feel that the people were praying during the week for the upcoming services. We loved the people there, and we still hear from some of them. Also, we see many of them when we go to the Camp Meetings in Whittier, North Carolina.

"I will instruct thee and teach thee in the way which thou
shalt go: I will guide thee with mine eye" (Psalm 32:8).

Chapter Thirty Nine

THE HOUSE THAT WOULDN'T BURN

We had a fire at our house just three days after moving into the parsonage at Bryson City, North Carolina. It was around ten o'clock on a Saturday night, and I was drying the fourth load of clothes I had washed. I was also ironing the clothes that we would be wearing for our first service at our new church.

We could hardly walk through the house because of all the boxes that remained unpacked in every room. All day, I had unpacked boxes in the kitchen and put up dishes, pots and pans, and groceries.

Suddenly, Larry came through the hallway saying that he smelled something burning. He looked into the laundry room near the kitchen and saw flames coming from the back of the clothes dryer. I remember him saying frantically, "How do you turn this thing off?" and "GET ME SOMETHING, GET ME SOMETHING!" Then he opened the dryer door and yanked the sheets out and threw them into the hallway. We couldn't find the fire extinguisher that we had seen in the house earlier, so our teenage son, Scott, ran down the hill to the church to find one. I remember saying "I plead the Blood, I plead the Blood (of Jesus)" just before I went to the phone to dial 911. Help arrived within a few minutes.

The sheriff's deputy arrived first and turned off the breaker (Why didn't we think of that?). Then the fire truck and some volunteer firemen came soon after that. Some of our new church members arrived within minutes also, and stayed with us throughout the ordeal. The firemen and sheriff's deputy could never have found our house if

Scott had not been down at the church to point to the steep hill which led up to our house. You could barely see that there was a house up there.

The flames were still visible when the deputy arrived, but the fire stopped when he turned off the breaker. They pulled the dryer out of the house and opened windows and doors to let the smoke out.

My husband watched as the deputy touched the walls around where the dryer had been, and he heard him say in utter amazement, "THIS WALL IS NOT EVEN WARM!" There were no burned places on the wall or ceiling or on the shelves above the dryer. The fire did *absolutely no damage* to the house at all! The vinyl floor under the dryer had a tiny cut in it that was made when the firemen pulled the dryer out of the laundry room, but other than that, no damage had occurred.

As it turned out, there was a build-up of lint and some old socks (left by the former pastor's family) underneath the dryer and they caught fire when the dryer overheated from hours of use that afternoon and evening.

We were able to sleep in the house that night, and the smell of smoke vanished quickly. There was no smoke damage at all. We went to our first service at church the next morning, thanking God for His wonderful protecting power. We praised Him for the power in the Blood of Jesus. We saw firsthand that God still works miracles today!

"The angel of the Lord encampeth round about them that fear him, and delivereth them" (Psalm 34:7).

CHAPTER FORTY

HEARTS, HEARTS EVERYWHERE

In June of the year 2000, while we were living at Bryson City, North Carolina, I began to notice that I was seeing hearts and valentines constantly. An anniversary card came first—in the shape of a heart. Then my Sunday School lesson that I was studying to teach the children had a big picture of a heart in it. Soon after that, the children of the church came up to me after church to give me some pictures they had drawn just for me, and the pictures had hearts all over them. Then, at Christmas, someone from the church gave us a wooden clock with hearts on it. All through the rest of that year and into the year 2001, hearts and valentines seemed to be put in front of my face constantly. I knew the Lord was showing me something, so I kept all this in mind.

Then, during the first few months of 2001, our son, Chris, found the girl of his dreams, Crystal Shepherd, and he told us that they were going to get married in June. They said they were planning to have the wedding at the *Heartland* Wedding Chapel in Townsend, Tennessee.

Also, a short while before Chris and Crystal met each other, I saw in my mind while I was praying, a ring (like an engagement ring up against a black velvet background, like you would see in a jewelry store). At the time, I wondered what that meant. The Lord knew exactly what was going to happen, and I believe He was trying to show me what was about to take place, but I didn't put it all together (the hearts, valentines, and ring) until Chris announced his engagement and mentioned the *Heartland* Wedding Chapel. Chris and Crystal were married in a beautiful ceremony there in the Great Smoky Mountains on June 2nd, 2001.

I still stand amazed that God showed us signs of things to come, even when it concerned the marriage of one of our children.

"How precious also are thy thoughts unto me, O God!
How great is the sum of them!" (Psalm 139:17).

CHAPTER FORTY ONE

GOD STILL HEALS TODAY

There have been countless times throughout the years when I would wake up during the night feeling sick, or I would be feeling bad at bedtime. I would ask Larry to pray for me, and within minutes I would begin to feel better and I would fall asleep immediately. The Lord has healed me many other times as well, but I recall two times within the last few years when the Lord brought healing to my body.

Four years ago (while we were pastoring the Bryson City Church of God), I decided to take the job of church custodian when that position became available. I just wanted to have some extra spending money. The church restrooms had just been remodeled, so I cleaned the new paneling, and got down on my hands and knees to scrub and clean the glue off the new flooring. Then, after only three months of weekly church cleaning, something happened to my hands. They became stiff and sore, and I developed what is called "trigger finger". One or more of my fingers on both hands would lock down and I could not get them pulled back up. It was very painful, and sometimes it would happen during the night, and I would wake up with my fingers locked down. I was concerned that I would lose the use of my hands and that I would not be able to play the piano or organ any longer, or even be able to type or write.

I went to a hand specialist in Asheville. He took X-rays, ordered blood work to check for rheumatoid arthritis, and he put splints on my fingers. Then he prescribed some pills with dangerous side effects, but I did not take the pills after I read the information sheet.

So, I told the doctor on the next visit that I had not taken the medicine, and that I had been fasting and praying for my healing. He seemed surprised, and then with his hands up, he said, "Whatever works!" My fingers and hands were healed within a short while, and I never went back to him again. Dr. Jesus took care of it!

Another healing came while we were pastoring at Reidsville, North Carolina. My right foot started hurting terribly, and I had trouble walking on it. I finally went to a foot specialist, and he diagnosed the trouble as bursitis. He put shots in my foot on two different occasions, but that did not seem to help. I decided not to go back to the doctor for more torture, and to just trust the Lord for my healing. I was not disappointed! I had to wait on the Lord a while, but complete healing did come. I praise the Lord for His wonderful healing power!

"Behold, God is mine helper . . . ." (Psalm 54:4a).

Chapter Forty Two

THE GRAY HOUSE

After we had pastored the Bryson City Church of God for almost two years, we began to feel that it was time to go elsewhere. We prayed and sought the Lord about it, and then talked to our State Overseer about a change of pastorates. Later, our State Overseer called, and mentioned the Cashiers Church of God in Cashiers, North Carolina. We drove the 50 miles over to Cashiers to look around. We had never been there before. It was a nice little town nestled high up in the mountains. At first, we drove right past the church and parsonage, but then turned around after we spotted the church van in the parking lot.

When I saw the parsonage, I realized that it was the house I had seen in a vision five years before while we were pastoring at Hazelwood, North Carolina. I had been on the floor, praying in an extra bedroom in the Hazelwood parsonage, and I saw a vision of a gray house with a porch in the middle of the front of the house. I didn't know what it meant at the time, but I was so amazed about the vision, that I drew a picture of the house and wrote down what I saw. I mentioned the color of the house and that there seemed to be an extra door on the side of the front porch. I eventually put the picture in a drawer and forgot about it.

But when I saw the parsonage at Cashiers, I knew it was the house in my vision, and I felt sure that this was where the Lord was going to send us. I went home and searched the house for the picture I had drawn. When I found it, I was amazed to see how much the Cashiers parsonage looked like that house. (To my surprise, the house did have an extra door on the left side of the front porch leading to the laundry room and kitchen).

A short time later, the Cashiers church was allowed to vote for their new pastor, and our name was the only name considered, although we thought other names would be given to them. They voted for us to come there as their pastor, and we moved there just a week or so after that.

The Lord had led me to write down several words before going there, among which were "bear" and "fish." After moving to Cashiers, we quickly realized that the men of the church, as well as most men in that area, loved to go bear hunting. It was a popular pastime in that area.

Also, the men of the church really enjoyed fishing. They even went on an annual fishing trip together to Panama City, Florida. They would freeze the fish and have fish suppers at someone's house or at the church, just for fellowship. Those were good times.

We had an enjoyable time at the Cashiers church, and the people worked with us very well. It was a small congregation, and we hoped and prayed that we would see great growth and better results there, but we only saw a limited growth. Only eternity will tell what we accomplished at Cashiers—preaching, teaching, singing, and visiting for 15 months. I trust that our ministry was a blessing to the people there.

"But there is a God in heaven that revealeth secrets . . . ."
(Daniel 2:28).

CHAPTER FORTY THREE

GOD'S GUIDANCE FOR OUR SON

A few years ago, our oldest son, Steve, was seeking for direction from the Lord about whether or not he should relocate with his job. He was really happy with his job, but his boss was putting a lot of pressure on him to move from the Atlanta area to Pensacola, Florida. Steve really enjoyed living in the Atlanta area and he was very active and involved with his church there. At that time, he could not bear the thought of leaving his church and his friends. We were praying earnestly for him, that God would lead and guide him.

Then one Sunday at his church, he went forward for prayer during the altar service, and when the minister prayed for him, he was slain in the Spirit. (For readers who may not understand this, sometimes a person will fall backwards on the floor, under the mighty power of God, when a Spirit-filled person prays for them). While lying on the floor, he felt that the Lord was speaking to him and telling him he should stay in the Atlanta area instead of moving to Pensacola. Steve said he felt that the Lord was also saying that He would give him a better job in the Atlanta area. So, feeling that the Lord had definitely given him directions to stay and wait on Him, he told his boss that he could not move to Pensacola. Shortly after that, a *better* job did indeed open up for Steve in the Atlanta area.

Several years later, Steve began to feel led to move to Sarasota, Florida, where he had graduated from high school. By this time in his life, he was ready for a change. He prayed earnestly for an open door for employment there, and the Lord heard and answered, giving him a good job in Sarasota. The Lord has blessed him and helped him, I believe, because he prays and seeks God for guidance, and because he has always given generously to the Lord's work. It is comforting to know that God always keeps His promises and that He takes good care of His own!

> "Thou shalt guide me with thy counsel, and afterward
> receive me to glory" (Psalm 73:24).

CHAPTER FORTY FOUR

GOING TO BETHEL

Chickens, pottery, quilt, and key . . . These are just a few of the words the Lord impressed me to write down before we moved to the Bethel Church of God.

We had only been pastoring the Cashiers Church of God (in the Smoky Mountains of North Carolina) less than 15 months when we started feeling that maybe God wanted us to move. The church people there were so very nice to us and we did love them dearly. However, we kept feeling that it was time for us to move elsewhere. I wrote down the words the Lord would give me, one by one, at different times over a period of several months, and we just waited to see what each word would mean in our future.

We talked to our State Overseer and told him about the fact that we were feeling led to make a change. Then, in November of 2002, we received a phone call from our State Overseer's secretary asking if we would be interested in going to preach for the people at the Bethel Church of God in Seagrove, NC. Their pastor had retired and they were seeking a new pastor. They wanted to hear several ministers preach before making their decision. We consented to go, and we felt very excited about it. Again, fasting and prayer played a part in God's guidance for our lives. We truly wanted His will to be done. During the fast, I kept seeing scripture verses and other things, over and over again, about hens and chickens. I told Larry, "The Lord is trying to show us something about chickens." Also, I had been seeing things about pottery.

We had heard in the past that Seagrove, NC had some pottery places, but as we drove to the church that Wednesday afternoon (a four and a half hour trip), we were shocked beyond belief when we saw signs for various pottery shops every few feet, as we neared the area where the Bethel church was located. There were **hundreds** of pottery shops around Seagrove! They had recently attached new signs underneath the 705 Highway signs, calling it the Pottery Highway. I was praising God with all my heart after we started seeing the pottery shops and signs. I knew He was leading us to go there.

We had a wonderful service that night! The church was full and you could literally feel the excitement in that sanctuary. They were having choir singing that night, and I went to the choir to join in. I thought my heart would burst as they sang the songs with such a powerful anointing! I sang a solo that night and Larry preached. We had a time of questions and answers after the altar service, so they could get to know us better. I remember that some of the ladies were holding onto my arms after church, trying to show that they loved us.

When we talked to the church clerk after the service, he began to tell us about the different members and how they were employed. He mentioned nurses and school teachers, and he added that, along with another business, he raised **chickens**. He said he had about 50,000 of them! His dad (the Sunday School superintendent) also raised chickens, as did the choir director (about 70,000 of them)! When he said the word "chickens," I knew we were in the right place! Within a few days, Larry was chosen to be the new pastor at the Bethel Church of God, and we moved there about two weeks before Christmas, in 2002.

The ladies of the church were getting ready to do a fund-raising project using a handmade **quilt** that had been donated for that purpose. Also, soon after our arrival, our clerk and his wife invited us to their house for dinner, and they had a beautiful quilt hanging on the living room wall as a decoration. This offered me reassurance that we were in the right place.

Then I started wondering why the Lord gave me the word "key." Would you believe the truck that brought heating oil to the church was from the **Key** Oil Company? Only God could know all of these things in advance. He is such an awesome God!

After we had been there for a few weeks, I began to feel so incapable to fill the shoes of the former pastor's wife, Sister Lou Beaver. Someone had told me that she was like "the Energizer Bunny," always busy doing things for the church. Also, there were so many talented ladies there, and I felt that I just wasn't good enough to be the pastor's wife there. I know now that Satan was causing me to feel that way. I was feeling overwhelmed with these thoughts, but no one knew how I was feeling except for Larry. Then one Sunday at church, the former pastor (Rev. Terry Beaver), came up to me to tell me something. He said, "Sister Hemphill, God just wants you to BE YOURSELF!" I knew immediately that God had revealed to him what I was feeling, and He gave Brother Beaver the words I needed to hear. Those negative feelings left right then, and God filled me with confidence to go forward with our work at Bethel.

We were so very happy while pastoring the Bethel Church of God! The people were so wonderful to us, and we had great singing and great services while we were there. We were astounded at how the Lord blessed the church in many ways during our four years and one month there, especially with the finances. We loved pastoring the Bethel church and having fellowship with the people there. How we miss our friends at Seagrove!

Larry retired from pastoring churches after our time at Bethel, but he still preaches often at the church where we attend. He also preaches at various churches elsewhere and conducts funeral services when asked. I want to mention here that Larry has always taught and preached scriptural holiness. We adhere to the scripture in Hebrews 12:14 where it reads: "Follow peace with all men, and *holiness,* without which no man shall see the Lord." Also, we have always believed that one should pay tithes and give offerings to the church. Giving to World Missions was another thing we encouraged because we know that God always blesses a church or an individual when they give to missions. God gave us many financial miracles throughout our lives after giving to missions, to His church, or to people in need.

I will always enjoy telling about instances of God's miracles and His ways of leading and guiding us or making known His will by giving us unusual signs. He can do the same for you!

"That all the peoples of the earth may know the hand of
the Lord, that it is mighty." (Joshua 4:24).

CHAPTER FORTY FIVE

ANGELS ALL OVER MORGANTON

A short while before Thanksgiving in 2003 (while we were still at Seagrove), I had a dream that I did not understand at the time. I dreamed that I saw a little girl holding a picture she had drawn, and she came up to me to show me the picture. She had drawn little things all over the page, but I could not tell what they were. I asked her what they were, and she said, "They are angels all over Morganton." I had been through Morganton many times on trips and we knew the pastor of the Church of God there, but why I would dream about Morganton, I just did not understand. I thought maybe the Lord wanted me to call the pastor's wife there and tell her that there were angels all over their city. That would certainly be encouraging to any pastor and his family! But I decided maybe the dream didn't mean anything at all, so I dismissed it from my mind. It wasn't until after Thanksgiving that I realized the significance of the dream.

Our three sons, Steve, Chris, and Scott, (and Chris' wife, Crystal) came to our house in Seagrove to eat Thanksgiving dinner with us, and to stay for a few days. After seeing Saturday's weather forecast on Friday afternoon, Scott, who was a college student at that time, decided that he needed to go back to Cleveland, Tennessee, that night to get ahead of the snow storm that was predicted. He left that afternoon. He told us later that when he got to Morganton, North Carolina, it started snowing very hard and he had a struggle trying to travel in those conditions for several more hours. He had to travel through the Great Smoky Mountains and around a dangerous gorge in Ocoee, Tennessee. Fortunately, the weather was not very bad when he reached that area. The Lord was merciful and helped him to get home safely. We had prayed for his safety, and I am sure he was praying also. After he told us that he was in Morganton when he encountered the heavy snow, I knew then that the dream did have significance.

Although it was not until after Scott's trip back to Cleveland that we realized what the dream meant, we believe God was trying to show us ahead of time that his angels would be all over Morganton waiting for Scott to come through there in the snow, and to keep him safe the rest of the way home! After that, every time we would travel through Morganton on the expressway, I thought about the dream and praised God for his protecting power. Oh, what a wonderful God we serve!

"Let all the earth fear the Lord: let all the inhabitants of the world stand in awe of him" (Psalm 33:8).

CHAPTER FORTY SIX

TWO MIRACLES OF HEALING

My husband, Larry, has had two miracles of healing that stand out in my mind. The first was in Cherokee, North Carolina a few years ago while we were there for a Western North Carolina Minister's Meeting. We went to a reception at the Holiday Inn to welcome our new State Overseer. A service was planned at the campground nearby in Whittier immediately following the reception.

Fruits and various other foods were served at the banquet. We got our food and found a place to sit. After about five minutes, Larry began to choke on some of the food. One of the ministers helped him to the rest room and tried to do the Heimlich maneuver, but the piece of food remained lodged in his throat. He could still breathe and talk, but he was obviously in distress.

The people at the motel desk out front could not find anyone to help, but offered to call an ambulance. We declined the offer and headed out the door. I was going to drive him to the Sylva Hospital nearby. But on our way to the car, we saw a minister and his wife that we knew, and we hurriedly told them what was happening. Right there in the parking lot, this minister laid his hand on Larry's shoulder and prayed the prayer of faith. Immediately, the piece of food dislodged from Larry's throat! All four of us began to praise God, and there was no need to go to the hospital! We went on to the tabernacle at Whittier and enjoyed the service that night.

The second miracle came in January of 2004 during a Wednesday night service during our pastorate at the Bethel Church of God in Seagrove, North Carolina.

Larry had some dizziness and blurred vision before he got up to preach, but he did not tell me about it. He felt better after a few minutes, so he went on to the pulpit to preach at the appointed time. He read his Scripture verses, announced his text, and prayed. As he proceeded to preach and read other Scripture verses, he had trouble saying the words. I knew something was wrong, but it seemed that I was frozen in my seat. I sat on the edge of the pew just waiting for him to get all right and continue preaching, but he couldn't. He looked at a certain man and was going to ask him to pray, but he couldn't call the man's name. I said it for him. Then he asked several different people to testify, but he told me later that he had trouble remembering their names.

Still standing behind the pulpit, he managed to ask everyone to come to the altar. The men of the church quickly gathered in the front and asked him to come and let them pray for him. The whole church came around the altar and prayed earnestly for him, and God touched him! He was able to think and speak without trouble after the prayer.

I took him across the street to our house as soon as church was dismissed. I suggested going to the emergency room, but he refused. We went to the doctor the next morning and also for an MRI later on, but no trouble was found. We just thank God for His healing touch that night!

".... and with his stripes we are healed" (Isaiah 53:5b).

CHAPTER FORTY SEVEN

NO SNOW

After Larry retired from pastoral work, he was invited to preach at the Berryton Church of God in Summerville, Georgia for a Sunday morning service on March 1, 2009. We really felt like the Lord wanted us to go and preach there, and for several weeks we had been excited about going there for the service. A friend of ours was the pastor of the church.

The weather forecasters were predicting heavy snow over all of North Georgia for that day. As the weekend neared, I felt like I should fast all day on Saturday about the weather, and we prayed earnestly for the Lord to make a way for us to go to the service on Sunday. While getting ready the next morning, we saw on the news that snow was falling heavily in Alabama and Tennessee, but it had stopped abruptly at the Georgia state line, near Summerville. We went on to our appointment that morning, and never saw a snowflake!

The pastor's wife was so disappointed because she wanted to see some snow! We heard people talking about how it was snowing in North Georgia up above where we were, and that it was snowing hard around the Atlanta area (which was below where we were). After the service, we went to lunch with the pastor and his wife at a restaurant in Summerville. Then I called my mother in Marietta to see how the weather was at their house. She said they had about 3 inches of snow and it was still snowing heavily.

We headed home and never saw snow falling all the way home, but we did see a dusting of snow on the ground when we got back to Cobb

County and also in our yard in Paulding County. The roads remained clear on the entire path that we had to travel that day! Only eternity will tell what was accomplished in the service that day at the Berryton Church of God. We just know that God wanted us there for a special reason.

Looking at the weather map later on television, we saw that the snow fell on the east side of where we traveled, on the north side, the west side, and south of us, but there was a "pocket" that received no snow at all. That "pocket" was the area that we had traveled to get to our preaching engagement! We serve a miracle-working God! Praise His name!

> ". . . great things doeth he, which we cannot comprehend"
> (Job 37:5b).

Chapter Forty Eight

MISCELLANEOUS EXPERIENCES

We were traveling home to Seagrove in the early hours of the morning after a vacation trip. While going through Greensboro, I noticed that Larry was getting very sleepy and tired after driving for a long time. I offered to drive the rest of the way home, since I was wide awake. I had been praying and worshiping the Lord silently on the way home, and I was feeling happy and joyful. So we pulled over and switched places. After driving for about fifteen minutes or more, suddenly, two large deer ran out into the road in front of us. I had no time to think about what to do. Normally, I think I would have slammed on the brakes or swerved to one side, but instead, I drove straight ahead at the same speed as before, and I DROVE RIGHT BETWEEN THE TWO DEER! Neither one of them touched our car. Larry and I were both totally amazed at what had happened and we started thanking God for protecting us.

A second thing I wanted to share was when I dreamed that I was sitting on the side of a bed holding a beautiful baby girl. She was facing the door behind me, and when Larry walked through that door and into the room, she looked at him and said, "Pap-paw!" Not too long after that, Scott and Whitney told us that they were expecting a baby—our first grandchild. A few months later, our beautiful granddaughter, Lily Grace, was born!

On another occasion, I dreamed one night that I was looking at an electric switch on the wall. It seemed that a voice was saying, "Switch means swap." Soon after that, we "swapped" churches with another pastor in a different state.

The next thing I wanted to share was when I woke up suddenly one night after dreaming something about a famous evangelist and an airplane. I felt troubled and started praying for him, thinking that maybe he would be in an airplane crash or something like that. A short time later, we saw on the news that this evangelist was in deep trouble of another kind, and they showed him coming down the steps of an airplane. We were saddened by the news, because we had enjoyed his preaching and his music for many years prior to that time. Thankfully, today his ministry has been restored.

In addition, I wanted to tell about how the Lord gave me the word "popcorn" before Larry retired from pastoral ministry. I thought this was strange, but I wrote it down and waited to see what it would mean. Then, after we moved back to Georgia and started looking for a church to attend, we visited several churches to see which one we liked. We prayed and asked the Lord to show us where we should attend. We visited the Celebration Church of God several times, and each Sunday in their church bulletin, I noticed that they were promoting an upcoming event for the young people—a night to watch a video and have popcorn! And, it had a picture of a bag of popcorn beside the announcement. I knew then that this must be the church we should attend. We saw later that they have a popcorn machine in the church kitchen also. Of course, this is not the only reason we chose to attend this church! The anointed preaching and the beautiful choir singing were the things that drew us in. Most important of all, we could feel the presence of the Lord in the services. As it turned out, we received a warm welcome at the church, and we have had many opportunities to preach, teach, and sing during our six and a half years at the church. We have made many good friends there also. God knew ahead of time where we needed to be!

Finally, another strange thing happened during the week of March 2, 2009. I was lying in bed one morning half awake and half asleep when I heard someone calling out "Momma.". Since that is what my children would call me when they were little, I felt like one of my children must need prayer, so I started praying for our three sons immediately.

I found out that day that my dad fell in the bathroom that very morning at his house, and was in the floor calling out "Momma! Momma!" trying to get my mother's attention. (He called her "Momma" all the time). She couldn't hear him at first because she was in the kitchen and the television was on nearby. Finally, she heard him calling out and ran to see about him. She couldn't get him up by herself, so she called for help to get him up. He was not hurt at all and we thank God for that.

The amazing thing is that I heard someone calling "Momma" before he ever fell that morning, and before he ever called out for help. I knew that someone needed help, but I didn't know who it was. I did pray, and I believe God heard my prayer and protected him from getting hurt, even though I misunderstood who was calling out for help.

". . . stand still and consider the wondrous works of God"
(Job 37:14b).

CHAPTER FORTY NINE

DOES THE STORY END HERE?

No! I am glad to say that our story does not end here. We have been retired from pastoral ministry for six and a half years now, and the Lord is continuing to show us things and to lead and guide us by His Spirit day by day.

God performed miracles when I had to undergo two major colon surgeries within three months time. The Lord was really with me during this trying time, and even though cancer was suspected, no cancer was found! We just can't praise Him enough for the miracles that took place during this time of illness.

Larry was healed of a severe backache on the morning that he was scheduled to preach at the Temple Church of God. He was in bad shape with his back on Saturday and it looked as if he would not be able to go to the church to preach the next day. Once again, prayer and fasting was our course of action all day on Saturday, and he woke up on Sunday morning completely healed! I remember that he suddenly ran down the middle aisle of that church when testifying of how the Lord had healed his back so he could be there to preach that day!

The Lord has opened many doors of opportunity for Larry to preach at different churches here in Georgia, as well as in North Carolina, since he retired from pastoral work. We have also been active in our church. Larry preaches there often, and I sing in the choir, and sing solos from time to time.

The Lord has made it possible for me to do substitute teaching in the schools near our house in Powder Springs, Georgia. He has helped me tremendously with this. Also, along with this job, I worked at The School Box for almost three years. I am continuing to write new songs and sending them off to be published or recorded.

We thank God for helping our three sons and their wives, and we are believing God to work many wonderful miracles in their lives in the future.

We are praising the Lord also for our four grandchildren, Lily, Locke, Levi, and our newest (but oldest) grandson, Mateo, who joined our family when Steve and Adriana married in May of 2012. We enjoy spending time with our sweet grandchildren!

On June 23rd, 2012, Larry and I celebrated 50 wonderful years of marriage! We renewed our vows that day at the Trinity Fellowship Church where Larry's brother, Richard, is the pastor. Rev. Keith Graham, our pastor, performed the ceremony. My parents walked me down the aisle! All three of our sons participated by giving a tribute to us during the service. Also, Scott sang a solo (a sweet love song) for us. All this was followed by a beautiful reception in the fellowship hall. We were so happy to be joined by many relatives and friends on our special day. I am so thankful that my daddy lived to see that day. I never dreamed that he would go home to be with the Lord less than a year later.

As I write this, we have already celebrated our 51st anniversary. We are so blessed! We look forward to all the miracles God will perform in our future as we fast and pray. I plan to record it all and, hopefully, write about it later. I can't wait to see what He will do!

> "Ah Lord God! behold, thou hast made the heaven and the earth by thy great power and stretched out arm, and there is nothing too hard for thee" (Jeremiah 32:17).